Affiliate Marketing:

Beginners Guide to Learn Step-by-Step How to Make Money Online using Affiliate Program Strategies and Earn Passive Income up to $10,000 a Month

Daren H. Russell

Table of Contents

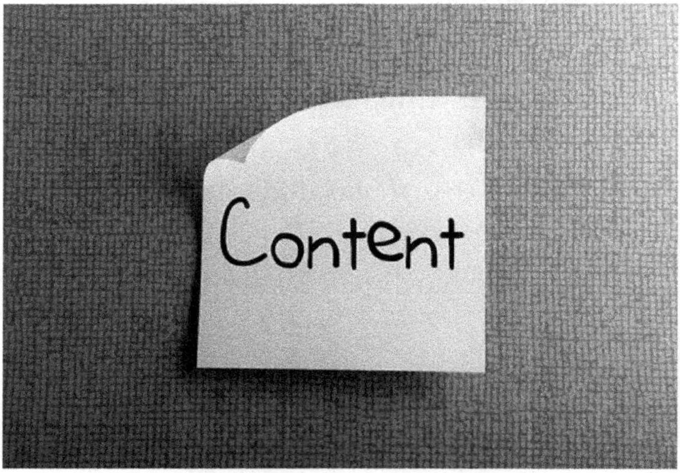
Content

Introduction:

We all want more money than we have now; we simply can't get enough of the stuff! But, for many people, the daily slog of getting up, getting ready, leaving the house, spending several hours in an airless office or doing the same job over and over, before returning home, is fast becoming an undesirable way to make that money.

What if I were to tell you that there is another way? What if I were to tell you that you could make serious money without leaving home without even having to get dressed in the morning? Well, that is exactly what I am going to tell you and, what's more, I will even tell you, step by step, how to do it! All you need are a computer, a stable and fast internet connection and a passion for hard work because this won't be easy; this method is not a get-rich-quick scheme without putting in the hard work that goes with it.

Welcome to my guide on affiliate marketing. Yes, that's right – affiliate marketing. No doubt you have heard people slating this kind of marketing as a complete waste of time but I'm going to show you that it is far from that. It is only a waste of time if you think that you can get something for nothing.

Setting up for affiliate marketing will take time and it will take many hours but look at it this way – that time and those hours can be spent in the comfort of your own home. No more rising to the alarm clock to get to work on time; no more battling the traffic or listening to the inane chatter of a bunch of robots on a train and no more having to put up with annoying irritating co-workers.

This is your time; this is all about you showing you that you can do it, that you have what it takes to be a successful affiliate marketer and that you can pull in the big bucks. Throughout this guide I will be explaining everything you need to know to be successful. We'll start by looking at what affiliate marketing is and how it works before we move on to the nitty-gritty. At the end of each chapter, I'll give you a Quick Start Action Step, a simple step that gets you on the move and working towards your ultimate goal very quickly. And I will also tell you what NOT to do if you want to succeed.

Are you ready to change your life for the better? Then get comfortable in front of your computer and start working through my guide right now.

Chapter 1: Getting Started with Affiliate Marketing

What is Affiliate Marketing?

Affiliate marketing is one of the most popular methods used today for making money online. Affiliates market products and services for other companies and people, earning commission on any sales that are made directly through their marketing efforts. It sounds difficult but it is actually quite straightforward; an affiliate will find a product that they want to market and will promote it in a way that makes others want to buy it.

Affiliate marketing is something that has long been associated with the internet but it is happening everywhere and has done since long before the internet was even thought of. Think about any time when a company provides a discount to an existing customer for introducing new customers – that is affiliate marketing but people don't tend to think of it that way.

When the internet was invented, we were all connected to everybody else all of a sudden and that is when affiliate marketing really began to take off. No more were you restricted to an area to sell or buy goods in; now you could sell to anyone and thus began a series of brand new techniques for marketing.

In 1989, William J Tobin was granted the patent for affiliate marketing, the first person to set up a marketing program for his own company called PC Flowers & Gifts. Their affiliate marketing program was aimed at a floral company we know today as FTD, and Tobin was responsible for laying the groundwork that makes up today's affiliate marketing; it may have changed as each year passes but the core concept is exactly the same.

It was when cookies were invented that the face of affiliate marketing changed forever. Cookies are small bits of data that track you and what you do and this tells third-parties a little bit about how you use their website. For affiliate marketing purposes, companies could now track even more, including whether a marketing campaign was working or not.

The first affiliate networks, ClickBank and Commission Junction, started in 1998 and today they are still the most popular networks ever. These are the networks that allow the small businesses not featured on Amazon to get their foot in the affiliate door, expanding how far they could reach and allowing others to get paid for helping them. Today there are many more affiliate networks available, with the business evolving as the internet evolves and, for some people, affiliate marketing is where they make they fortune.

Top Affiliate Marketers

There are thousands of people who have made their money through affiliate marketing and some of the best marketers that you should pay attention to are:

- **Pat Flynn** – Started his business in 2008, taking over a year to build his website and earning $8000 as his first income. By 2013, that had risen to over $50,000 per month.
- **John Chow** – Like Flynn, Chow started from nothing and today his affiliate business also brings him in more than $50,000 per month, claiming he works just 2 hours per day.
- **Jeremy Schoemaker** – Starting his blog in 2003, Schoemaker went on to launch affiliate market services for eBay and Auction Ads. The most viewed photo of Schoemaker is one of him holding a check from Google AdSense for more than $32,000 and it is estimated that, in just 5 years, he earned between $2,000,000 and $4,000,000.

There are many more affiliate marketers out there but these are just three that you should follow and learn from – they all started from nothing and this book is aimed at helping you learn how you can use affiliate marketing to start from nothing and earn your own passive income.

Why Affiliate Marketing?

Why not? There are loads of ways that you can apparently make money on the internet but affiliate marketing is one of the most tried, tested and proven methods there is. Thousands of businesses and e-commerce stores can testify to just how efficient it is and just about anyone can do it, although many do fail. In chapter 3, I will tell you why they fail so you don't make the same mistake.

So why would you choose affiliate marketing anyway?

- **It's a great way to earn money from products that are already selling.** Businesses need advertising to get the word around about their product and to boost profit and that is where you, the affiliate comes in. If you have a blog or a website already, you can use it to earn you some cash by advertising other people's products. You always go for the well-known names and brands because they already sell well and it doesn't take much to get people to buy them – it doesn't take too much effort to advertise them either. Use the popularity of these products to gain customers on your website, pass them to the main seller and reap the rewards in commission, what could be easier? One thing I do need to make clear here – you will read all sorts of stuff that tells you to pick products that you like. This does not work, unless the products you like are what your audience likes too. Anything your market must be aimed squarely at their tastes not yours.

- **It's far easier and cheaper than building a company from scratch.** That costs big money and you have no guarantees of success. Plus, when you have your own business, you need to make your own products. That requires planning, experimenting, drafting, and many more processes, all of which take time. Your products need to be tested and proven if they are to gain interest and there are far more responsibilities. With affiliate marketing, you sell something that someone else has already produced, marketed and built up a good name for are what sell, as well as quality.

- **It's far easier than most jobs.** There are four main processes to affiliate marketing, none of which is that complicated. You sign up to an affiliate program, more than one if you want. You then build an affiliate site and, using the affiliate tracking link you were supplied with, you connect that site to the main site of your chosen company. Visitors come to your site, they click a link and hopefully they make a purchase. You then get the reward in the form of commission. One thing you do need, though, is flexible and updated marketing skills and techniques – this job does need a little help from you!

- **Profit is quite quick to come.** Unlike making and selling your own product, with affiliate marketing, you reap the rewards much quicker. With affiliate marketing, you don't need to invest much money, simply time, knowledge and effort.

Pick the right companies and the right products, establish your own website or blog, keep your marketing skills up to date and keep your eye on the ball. That is what you need to be a successful affiliate marketer.

Affiliate Networks and Forums

Affiliate marketing is one of the biggest online industries that creates a steady income for millions of people. Before you choose your affiliate network, you should get yourself acquainted with who's who, the best of the best. Cast your eyes over these affiliate networks:

1. **CJ Affiliate by Conversant**

CJ Affiliate started life as Commission Junction and remains one of the biggest and most popular of all affiliate networks. Most of the big-brand merchants use CJ Affiliate to list their products making CJ one of the small number one-stop shops online.

2. **Rakuten LinkShare**

Rakuten has been in the affiliate market business for several years now and is one of the oldest networks in operation today. Their profile is no longer as large as it once was but it is still a respectable network, offering affiliate marketers the option of automatic rotation through numerous banner ads; this takes away the burden of having to select and optimize ads manually.

3. **Amazon Associates**

Amazon is, without a doubt, one of the biggest and most popular of all the affiliate networks, with more than 1.5 million sellers offering products, not to mention the many affiliates that are associated with the company. One of the biggest benefits is that Amazon Associates is very simple, with even complete beginners able to get a marketing scheme off the ground and running quite quickly. At the same time, marketers with plenty of knowledge can take full advantage of the APIs and implementation tools on offer from the network.

4. **ShareASale**

ShareASale is one of the biggest affiliate markets on the internet today, with a unique environment that very few other networks offer. ShareASale has around 3,800 merchants on file, with more than a thousand of those exclusive to the platform, and exclusive affiliates can only be seen by exclusive merchants, nowhere else on the internet. ShareASale also publishes data about their offers including reversal rates, income per click, average commission and much more.

5. **eBay Partner Network**

Very similar to what Amazon Associates offers, the eBay Partner Network is the perfect platform for bloggers or websites that specialize in one or two particular niches. On offer are a bunch of useful widgets and tools that can assist affiliates in earning even more commission. Where eBay Partner Network differs from Amazon is that, instead of offering a commission based on price, they offer a percentage of the eBay fees paid per sale. The network also has a 200% bonus on offer for any purchase form a new customer, which offers encouragement for new affiliates to push out to new audiences.

6. **CPA Affiliate Networks**

CPA Affiliate Networks is home to several providers, such as PeerFly and NeverBlue, both of which offer full access to options such as cost-per-action. These are ideal for dating websites, games and those that offer free trials of software. The cost-per-action approach will pay affiliates for actions and leads instead of sales with the result of conversion rates being much higher.

7. **Google Affiliate Networks**

Google has one of the largest presences online and this makes it an obvious choice for affiliate marketing. The idea behind the Google Affiliate Network is to assist marketers and advertisers to increase their traffic and make more conversions; it does this by offering a system based on performance whereby activity is monetized. With Google, you get a network that is pay-per-action, with commissions offered to affiliates who use leads and sales to drive conversions. You do require an AdSense account for posting the ads on your affiliate site and to help when it comes to payments.

8. **ClixGalore**

Based in Australia, ClixGalore is one of the international marketers. They also have offices in Japan, the UK, and the US too and, while their profile isn't so high as other networks, it does offer a solid service. Some of the biggest names appear on ClixGalore, including Trend Micro, Citibank, and Fox Sports Shop. Several types of program are on offer, including pay-per-lead, pay-per-impression and pay-per-sale. Most of the programs pay US dollars and affiliates can refer others to ClixGalore and earn a percentage of their referrals' earnings.

9. **ClickBank**

ClickBank was one of the first affiliate networks to be formed and is one of the most popular today. The primary merchants on ClickBank are digital, like membership websites, eBooks and software programs. Some products offer 75% commission and all commissions are paid weekly, with a direct deposit option available.

Affiliate Marketing Forums

These are a few of the best affiliate marketing forums to visit for help and advice:

1. **Warrior Forum**

Warrior Forum is one of the most interactive forums for affiliates and would-be affiliates to get involved in discussions and read reviews. It is also one of the best places to learn about new marketing trends and share experiences with others. The forum offers plenty of opportunities for discussing money making ideas and topics with plenty of advice on offer for newbies from old-hands in the business.

2. **SitePoint**

SitePoint is one of the more active forums, offering advice on affiliate marketing, internet marketing and more. It's a great place for affiliates to go for advice, with plenty of discussions on ideas.

3. **DigitalPoint**

DigitalPoint is one of the best places for affiliate professionals with plenty of ongoing discussions. You can get information and ideas on business, design, trade, development, search engines and more. You can also go on to join the DigitalPoint Marketplace and take part in buying and selling.

4. **The V7 Network**

The V7 Network is the perfect place for beginners to affiliate marketing to ask their questions and beef up on skills they need to learn. V7 is an active forum where people help one another to learn and there is always an answer to any problem. There are loads of active discussions that users can join in with.

5. **Affilorama**

Affilorama is a network that offers free training, help and support to beginners in the affiliate marketing world. They offer tools, training materials and full support kits to help you grow and learn what you need to know.

6. **WickedFire**

WickedFire is a crazy place but is a great affiliate marketing forum to get involved in. There is plenty of advice on offer that tells you how to earn money in a few alternative affiliation methods. But beginners beware – you need to be very aware of their engagement rules and in their culture before you join.

7. **AffiliateFix**

AffiliateFix is one forum designed especially for the beginner to affiliate marketing but experienced marketers are also very welcome, offering webinars, support, videos and more to help beginners get started. The big focus of the forum is to create new marketers as experts in their chosen areas.

8. **WebProWorld**

WebProWorld offers users a huge range of marketing areas to choose from, with discussions on all areas of affiliate marketing – search engines, IT, eCommerce, WebMaster, site design and more.

9. **ABestWeb**

ABestWeb is a great affiliate forum covering all the issues affiliate marketers face as well as information about SEO, IT and more. It is a professional forum and anything off-topic will be removed so, if you join, keep things to the point and very professional. This forum is all about sharing information and help, not about self-promotion.

10. **DNForum**

DNForum is incredibly rich as far as forums go, offering huge amounts of information and research including legal stuff, beginner guides, and all sorts of other information. When you join you get access to plenty of free resources as well as those that you pay for. There are also many Reddit users on the forum along with useful YouTube videos.

Quick Start Action Step

Schedule a slot in your diary, a minimum of 30 minutes, where you check out these affiliate networks and forums and learn as much as you can. At this stage, you are not choosing a network; all you want is ideas and information. Make plenty of notes; you will need them later.

Chapter 2: How Affiliate Marketing Works

How Does Affiliate Marketing Work?

So, we know what affiliate marketing is but how does it actually work? The idea is to promote the products that another company offers for sale. We all want to be able to wake up and look at an ever-growing bank balance, an account from Amazon or ClickBank of how many orders have been dispatched through your link and how much commission you've earned that day but there is only one way to do that – set yourself up as an affiliate marketer today. Here's how it works:

1. You set up as an affiliate marketer. You have your website or your blog and you've chosen your niche (more about that later).
2. You've chosen your affiliate network, having done your homework thoroughly, and you've chosen the products that you wish to promote. You have your affiliate

link and now it's time to start advertising.

3. You place your affiliate link/s through your website or blog in prominent places – I'll tell you how to do that later as well – and you wait.

4. When a visitor to your site clicks on one of your links, they are taken to the affiliate website where they can choose whether to make a purchase or not. If they do, great, you've earned yourself a tidy bit of commission; if they don't, you've lost nothing.

That all sounds quite simple, doesn't it? We can take this a little bit deeper and talk about the four main parties involved in affiliate marketing, just so you understand a little bit more. First, understand this – the affiliate marketing equation has two sides to it – the affiliate marketer and the creator and seller of the product. As such, affiliate marketing can be said to be a process of distributing the creation of a product and marketing that product across several different parties; each of those parties will receive a share of the profit as per their own contribution.

However, the creation of a product and promoting it are not the only things that define an affiliate marketer; you can create, you can market and you can make a profit from the idea of revenue-sharing. Now, back to those four parties:

- **The Merchant** is known by several other names – the brand, creator, retailer, seller, or vendor. Whatever name it is, this is the product creator, either a huge named brand or a small up and coming business. As a merchant, you don't even need to be actively involved in the affiliate marketing side of things; all you need is a product to sell.

- **The Affiliate** or the publisher. An affiliate can be one person or it can be a company and the potential to earn can run from a couple of hundred dollars per month right up to thousands, even millions of dollars in commissions. This is where the real work happens in affiliate marketing, with the affiliate promoting the product/s and attracting potential customers. It is the job of the affiliate to convince those customers that the product is worth buying and this is done through a website or a blog that reviews or mentions the products in a favorable way and includes links.

- **The Consumer** is the one that keeps the wheels turning. Without a consumer or a customer there are no sales and no sales means no commission. The affiliate markets their choice of products to the consumers in one or more of several ways. They may use social media, they may have a website or a blog, they may even use digital billboards. However they do it, it is down to the affiliate whether they let the consumers know that the links they promote are affiliate links. Most do; often you will see a notice on a blog stating that the content includes affiliate links and this is because the affiliate prefers transparency, prefers to let the consumer decide for themselves if they wish to make a purchase. All the consumer needs to know is that they are not paying any more for an affiliate product than they would if they purchased it through normal means.

- **The Network** is the fourth cog although not everyone considers them to be a part of the equation. Without the affiliate network, the affiliate doesn't have many options and they have to work much harder to find their products. The network is the middleman, the place where the marketer and the merchant are brought together. The network is much like a catalog where the affiliate gets to choose which products they want to market.

That is how affiliate marketing works in a nutshell; now we move on to a bit more detail about affiliate tracking (cookies) and the different types of payment arrangement to choose from.

How Does Affiliate Tracking Work?

One of the most important parts of affiliate marketing is tracking. When you generate a lead, it must be accurately accountable, in real-time and, very important, automatically. This tracking will tell the advertiser whether their affiliate campaign is working or not, and what needs to be ditched or fixed.

There are two main tracking types – conversion pixels and cookies and postback URLs. Which one you use will depend on what your affiliate program is

and what your own computing resources
are:

- **Conversion Pixels and Cookies**

When you join an affiliate program you
are given a unique affiliate ID and this is
included in your tracking links for the
products you are promoting. Whenever a
website visitor clicks that link, your
affiliate ID gets stored in their browser as
a cookie, which is a small text file. This
will stay in their browser for a certain
time period, normally around 30 days or
more or until the visitor clears it from
their history. So, let's say they click a link
of yours but don't follow through with the
purchase. Then, a couple of days later,
they change their mind and complete the
purchase. Because of that cookie, that
sale is still attributed to you and you still
get the commission.

Conversion pixels are small bits of code.
These are on the merchant webpage and,
whenever an action has been completed,
they will load. This could be a message

that thanks you for making a purchase or for registering. If the visitor has reached the page via an affiliate link and gets to the purchase confirmation page, this is tracked by the pixel as being a lead or a sale and, depending on the payment arrangement you have (we'll discuss those next), your commission is sent to your account.

Be aware that cookies are specific to browsers; should a visitor complete the sale using a different browser, you won't get paid because it can't be tracked.

- **Postback URLs**

This kind of tracking works on a server-to-server basis and is one of the most accurate ways to track links. However, it is a bit more involved than cookies. If an advertiser has offers on multiple affiliate networks they will generally use postback tracking. Information gets stored on the merchant's server which means that there isn't any code on the advertiser's website. When the affiliate link is clicked, the affiliate network will place an

ID tag in the advertiser's URL. When the visitor gets to the advertiser's landing page, the URL is updated with their ID. If that results in a sale or a lead being generated, the merchant's server will use the postback URL to send the information back to the affiliate network server.

Affiliate Marketing Payment Arrangements

When it comes to getting paid in affiliate marketing, you need to think very carefully about how you are going to do this because there are three main payment arrangements:

- **Pay-Per-Sale**

You will often see this called Cost-Per-Sale as well and one of the best examples of this kind of arrangement is the Amazon affiliate program. With this payment arrangement, the merchant will pay for any purchase made via an affiliate link. Some will pay a fixed commission amount while others, perhaps more commonly, pay a percentage of the sale figure.

- **Pay-Per-Click**

Also known as Cost-Per-Click. The merchant will pay an affiliate per the number of times a link is clicked to take a visitor to a merchant website. Be aware that only unique clicks will count so it's no good getting a mate to click repeatedly on a link; the clicks won't count and you risk being barred. The only thing that counts here is the click; the visitor is under no obligation to make a purchase and your earnings don't depend on purchases either.

- **Pay-Per-Lead**

Also known as Cost-Per-Lead. Companies that use this type of arrangement will make payments to an affiliate based on how many visitors referred by the affiliate go on to become leads, i.e. they sign up to the website. All they have to do is fill out a bit of information, usually an email address, which the merchant uses as a lead for sales or to sell on to a different company for them to use as a lead.

There are other arrangements in place as well. Any company can set up an affiliate program based on any action that would bring benefit to them and then make payments to their affiliates based on that action. In fact, there are two variations on the above schemes that you are likely to come across:

- **Two-Tier**

Two-tier affiliate programs are structured in much the same way as a network or multi-level marketing company, like Avon or Amway. The profit is made through the recruitment of sales staff and commission sales. As well as being paid commission for each sale, lead or click, the affiliates will also get a commission from the activity of any affiliate site that they refer on to the merchant.

- **Residual**

Affiliates who are in residual programs

can continually make a commission from one customer should that customer continue to make purchases from the merchant. The kind of online merchant that runs this type of program will be one who receives a regular payment from a customer, such as a monthly payment for a service.

In addition to all of this, there are some affiliate programs that work on something called Pay-Per-Impression. These are also known as Pay-Per-View and the affiliate will be paid based on how many visitors see the company banner ad. This doesn't usually tend to be structured like a standard affiliate program, more like an advertising program but there is one benefit to using it as an affiliate program – the merchant only pays when it gets the result it wants.

With traditional advertising, there is more of a risk because the advertiser is guessing how effective their ad will be and is paying up front. If it doesn't make back what it spent on the ad, they have to stomach the loss. And that is one of the main reasons why affiliate programs are so popular – the merchant only pays when they get the result they want, which is an incentive for the affiliate to go all out to advertise and promote their products.

Quick Start Action Step – Benefits of Affiliate Marketing

Take time out to read through these benefits and understand them. Write down, beside each one, whether you think it will benefit you and how. If you can think of any other reasons why you want to become an affiliate marketer, write them down too; at the end you should have a pretty impressive list that gives you the incentive you need to get started:

1. **You Are Your Own Boss**
And who doesn't want to work for themselves, to only have themselves to answer to? You decide when you want to work, you choose what you want to work on and you get to make all the decisions.

However, be aware that, as your affiliate marketing business grows, this will be quite a big responsibility but with that comes the rewards.

2. **Low Start-up Costs**

Normally, starting a business would cost a small fortune and you would have no guarantee of success. With affiliate marketing, the start-up costs are much lower – very affordable, in fact. All you need to pay out for is a domain name and web hosting if you don't already have them. WordPress is one of the best platforms to start a blog or website on; it's free and it has thousands of plugins that you can take advantage of, some free but some requiring payment. However, because of the low costs, affiliate marketing attracts a lot of people, raising the competition but doing it right will ensure that you reap the rewards ahead of them.

3. **It's Flexible**

We all like flexibility with our work and many of us place this ahead of financial gain. Working on the internet gives you that flexibility and working for yourself gives you the flexibility to work around your family and personal life. And, if you want to be an affiliate marketer as a second job, just to boost your income a little, you can easily do that. You are not tied to set times for working and, if you want, you can just work the evenings and weekends. That is true flexibility.

4. **No Need to Store Stock**

This is possibly one of the most attractive parts of affiliate marketing. You can sell as much as you want without ever having to handle stock. You don't need to concern yourself with keeping stock levels up, with packaging or with delivery. When you work on commission offline, you must manage all of that; with affiliate marketing online, the merchant deals with the details, leaving you to think about how to spend your commission.

5. **You Can Work from Anywhere**

So long as you have good internet, you could travel the world and still be an affiliate marketer. Once your business is off and running, it won't matter if you want to go off on holiday; it will pretty much look after itself.

6. **You Get to Learn New Skills**

As you learn to be an affiliate marketer you will learn some great new skills. If you are starting from scratch, you will learn how to build websites, you will learn SEO, conversion optimization, content marketing, managing social media, email marketing and a good deal more. Learning stuff by doing it is one of the best ways to really learn how to do something and, as digital skills are in really high demand right now, you can take this as far as you want.

7. **The Sky is Your Limit**

You can earn pretty much what you want to earn; put the work in and you will get the money out. Set aside time each day to work on your project and you will soon see the rewards start to grow.

Keep in mind that being an affiliate marketer is not going to be a five-minute job. You need to be truly committed as far as time goes if you want success. So many people think that affiliate marketing just requires setting up and then being left alone – while you can earn some money that way, you do need to keep on top of things. At the end of the day, it's like any project – the more you put in, the more you will get out.

Chapter 3: The Right Mindset to Succeed in Affiliate Marketing

Let's take a short break from talking about how affiliate marketing works and discuss what it takes to be successful at it. You see, anyone can be an affiliate marketer but 80 to 90% of those who start will fail. The reason why is very important to you. I am going to tell you what the most important thing is, the one thing that will determine whether you succeed or fail. And this one thing has nothing to do with the amount of traffic you drive in, it doesn't revolve around the number of conversions you make or the diligent work you did on keywords. What is that one thing?

Your mindset.

How you think will dictate what actions you take and that, in turn, will dictate what you do and when. I can hear some of you asking what on earth this has to do with affiliate marketing? I mean, you just want to get on and build that website and start watching the money roll in, don't you? Well, that's all well and good but if you don't approach this with the right mindset from the word go, I will tell you now, you are doomed to fail.

Get a piece of paper and a pen. Be very honest with yourself here; what do you consider to be important when it comes to affiliate marketing success? Write everything down that comes into your head. I guarantee you will have listed conversions, affiliates traffic and more and some of you will want to know what the best methods are to start making that money. And you want those methods right now but unless you get your mind on the right place, no method on earth is going to work.

Go into your affiliate marketing business with the attitude that you are going to succeed, come what may, and the chances are you will. Think the right way and you will find it much easier to implement a proper plan to take positive and proactive action that results in success. Think the right way and you will be able to solve any problem that gets in your way.

There are two types of approach to solving a problem – proactive and reactive.

- **Proactive** – your main thought is that you WILL succeed as an affiliate marketer and nothing is going to get in your way. When a problem arises, you will be proactive in finding the solution for it; you will use the search engines to look for the solution, you might head to YouTube or you might even go down the route of paying someone to solve it. Whichever you do, you are being proactive and not letting that issue get in your way.

- **Reactive** – you will be thinking, I'll just see if this works, if not I will give it up. When you encounter a problem, your first thought will be, "I can't fix this, it's too hard". You will turn your back and give it up as a bad job or you might turn to one of the many affiliate forums to complain about the problem; what you won't do is look for the solution. And then your mind starts to try to justify why you failed, to come up with excuse after excuse.

Are you starting to see where I am going with this? The only difference between these two is their mindset, the way they think. So, let's talk psychology for a while.

1. **Do not see affiliate marketing as a way of getting rich quickly.**
That is the one thing it isn't. You are not going to set up one day and find a fat check waiting for you the next day and every day after that. It just doesn't work that way. Affiliate marketing is a business and businesses only succeed with the correct strategy and planning in place.

2. **Know why you want to do it.**
This is where you need to start; to know

exactly why you want to do this. Once you have a clear and solid answer to that question in your mind, you are on the right track. Everyone wants to do it, everyone wants to know how to do it but how many actually know why? You might say that you want to make money but you have to want that badly enough. Whatever your reason is, it has to be enough to push you, to drive you forward all the time.

3. **Positivity is key**

So many times you will hear it said that you must have a positive mindset but, believe me, you will never hear it enough. Positivity is what keeps you moving forward, it keeps you motivated and it keeps your energy levels up. With the successes in affiliate marketing, you also get the setbacks and that is when you need your motivation. For some people, the setbacks, the lack of results, is enough to knock them back straightaway but this is the very time when you need that positivity.

4. You must have a business mindset

You must see affiliate marketing as a real business and for it to be successful, you must run it as such and that means having a business mindset. What does that mean? It means being prepared to invest money when needed, even if it is only a small amount – how much will depend on what your goals are and how big your marketing campaign is. Sometimes, you will need to invest in learning what to do next, how to take your business further and how to improve your system so it works. It is a business; run it that way and you have a much better chance of success.

5. You must be prepared to take action

Knowing something is one thing but taking action on it and doing something about it is quite another; if you don't take that action, your knowledge is useless and worthless. Too much time is spent on thinking and not enough on doing, do your thinking, get your ideas down on paper and then start putting action on them. Start doing or the money won't come and nobody else is going to do it for you.

6. **Cut the skepticism**

This is important. Many people start doing affiliate marketing but remain skeptical about it. They don't really think it can work but, hey, we'll give it a go anyway. Skepticism is what stops you from learning and earning. Think about it; anyone who searches for a way to make money online is skeptical about what they read and there is nothing wrong with a certain amount. It keeps you from falling for every scam there is. But not everything is a scam and provided you approach affiliate marketing the right way and choose only well-known affiliate networks to join then you won't be in any trouble.

Too much skepticism stops you from being successful; it can stop you from seizing on that one golden opportunity that could have made you for life. If you approach affiliate marketing in this kind of mindset, you won't get anywhere so be more open-minded, be prepared to learn and be prepared to fail; that way, you can find the way the right path to success.

So, now you know why you need to have a positive mindset to be successful at affiliate marketing but there is one more important thing to remember – I already said it once but I will say it again:

When you choose your products, don't go for what you like; go for what sells. Pick a successful niche and pick the products that people want to buy, not what isn't in demand. The reality of affiliate marketing is this; people are not interested in what you like. All they are interested in is whether the product works for them.

Chapter 4: Choosing the Right Niche

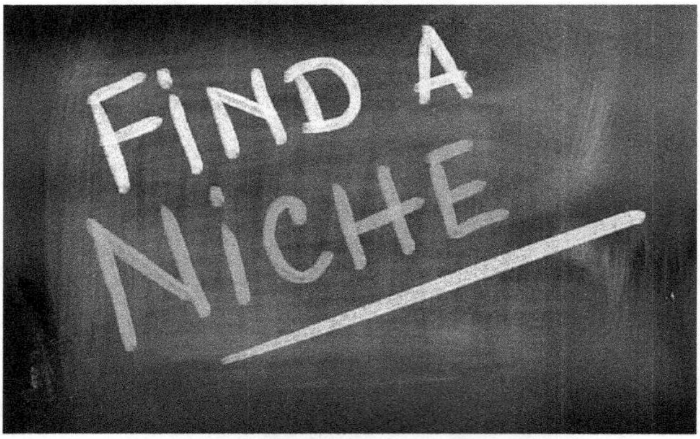
FIND A
NICHE

What is a Niche and Why Do You Need One?

One of the first things you need to do when you start your journey as an affiliate marketer is to choose your niche. This is the business area, the industry where you will focus your efforts and pick the products you want to promote. Essentially, it is your area of specialization. The key here is in focusing your efforts on one market rather than picking several and finding yourself getting frazzled trying to keep up.

Choosing your niche is a very important step and one of the biggest mistakes made by new affiliate marketers is that they don't narrow their niche down sufficiently. There are thousands upon thousands of affiliate marketers and bloggers out there today and they are all your competition; if you don't focus on a narrowed down area of the market, you will lose out.

You are going to see several completely different explanations of what a niche is as you do your research but the most common way of describing it is as a small and very specialized market segment. Or it could be defined as a group of people who are all searching for information or specific products. Both are correct and you should keep both in mind.

When you choose your niche, you are looking for that group of people you are finding them and the products or information that they want so badly to find. And when you find them, you will be giving them the information they want in a high-quality and informative manner and you will be providing them with easy links to the products they want through your affiliate link.

Benefits of a Niche for Affiliate Marketers

One of the biggest benefits of choosing a niche is that you get to establish yourself and your reputation as an expert in that area. People go to experts, they trust them, and if you are good enough, people will come to you for their information and they will go with your product or service recommendations.

When you pick a topic, avoid general ones as these won't get you noticed. A niche topic will put you in front of the right audience, will allow you to engage properly with them and, as a result, you can then build your followers up. Niche topics are far more involved because people feel as though sharing the same passions as others connect more closely to them.

The next benefit is affordability. Your advertising costs will much lower and your search engine rankings higher. When a person wants information on a specific topic they use specific terms to search for it, not general ones.

It isn't a requirement that you have an interest in your topic but it does help to keep you focused and motivated. You will also find it easier to write about and promote what you know because your knowledge will shine through. What you mustn't do is choose products in your niche that are based on what you like; choose the products that sell, the products that your audience wants. If you opt for a profitable niche that is NOT in your area of interest, be sure you do plenty of research before you publish any content – you must provide your audience with high-quality material that is highly relevant and up to date.

Choosing the right niche is the real key to affiliate marketing success and many opt for the bigger niches rather than choosing a smaller one. Why because they think that by going smaller, they are limiting the size of their audience and, as a result, their potential income. In practical terms, if you focus your efforts on a proper niche strategy, you will have a much higher chance of standing out and succeeding. Without any niche at all, your audience isn't really there; by knowing exactly who your target audience is, and being able to refine it as you go, will put you the right path. It doesn't matter if you choose one of the evergreen niches, such as recipes, health, lifestyle, etc., always start narrow and widen as you go.

Top 5 Affiliate Marketing Niches

The one question most asked by new affiliate marketers is, how do I find the right niche? There are thousands to choose from and knowing where to start can be quite overwhelming. If you want some advice, as a complete beginner, stick to one of the evergreen niches to start with; these have proved themselves time and time again to be the most profitable. The top five are:

1. **Finance**

This takes the top spot every year but before you dive in, think hard because finance is, without a doubt the toughest industry in affiliate marketing. There is an awful lot of competition here and, unless you have something truly unique, something that people really want but no-one else is offering, or you have something very special to bring to the market, you are going to find a new website or blog very hard to rank.

You can get in there but be prepared for it to take time. The only way to really break in is to be consistent – publish high-quality relevant blogs or posts, set up email marketing and even paid advertising and your business will start to grow.

2. **Health**

This is always going to be a popular niche because everyone has concerns about their health at some time or another; this makes it one of the best niches to start in. Promotion of products in the health niche has always yielded high revenue amounts and both Amazon and ClickBank offer plenty of products for you to work with.

3. **Web Hosting**

Web hosting will always be one of the

most lucrative industries for affiliate marketers, provided you do it correctly. Take WP Engine, a web host provider, for example; for every sale you make of their product, they will pay you $200 in commission. You don't need many of them in a week to start seeing the cash do you! The number of new websites and blogs that are set up daily is huge and web hosting demand will continue to grow to support that.

4. Technology

Another market that is rising fast is the technology market; technology is always going to be in demand, be it a smart TV, a mobile phone, the latest tablet and so on. Whatever it is, this is a market that you can get a serious foot in the door on and leverage to your benefit.

5. Romance

Bet you didn't expect to see this one here! Everyone wants romance in their lives and the topics under this niche stretch further than you could ever imagine possible. Think outside the box for this one – dating for the disabled, romance in an autistic world, and so on. And you also have the td and tested topics of improving relationships, dating tips, sexual health, dating for the single parent; you name it, you can write about it.

So, time to move on; let's look at how you choose and narrow down your niche.

How to Choose a Niche

Now you know what a niche is, why you need one and even what the top five are. Now it's time to look at how to choose one. Most affiliates will look at ClickBank or Amazon for their products and this is no bad thing. However, some niches are far more competitive than others so don't stick with just one or two affiliate networks to choose your products from; there are plenty of others.

1. The first thing you need to do is make a list of the topics you are interested in; don't be too focused

here, just write down everything and anything that you think you can do.

2. The second thing you are going to do is use the Google keyword tool. Open it and click the tab for **Search-Based Keyword Tool.** This is free to use for broad searches and, while it is generally used for inputting your website URL to find keywords, you can also use it to find niches.

3. When the tool opens, go to the bottom of the page and click on **Or See Top Keywords Across All Categories**

4. A new screen will open where you can see niche categories; open any one of them and you will see lots of sub-niches for each one. This is great data because it can really show you what people want, what they are searching for and you will also see, to the right of the niche

list, where the money is being spent.

5. Match the keywords on this list to what you have on your list and then go back to the Keyword tool and start typing! Input a phrase and see what comes up. For each one, you will see more keywords that are related, along with a volume of searches per month – obviously, the higher the number, the better it is.

6. Your next step is to work out whether a phrase is competitive enough to promote on a basic website. Go to the Google Search engine and type in that phrase – see what comes up. The hardest thing to do here is work whether a keyword is too competitive or not enough. As a rough idea, if you see more than 50,000 pages when you type a phrase inside quote marks in Google, try another one. You should also look at the top five

pages on the search results and see what's what on them.

7. Once you have narrowed your searches down to a couple of niches and you have a few keywords that you think are worth targeting, your next step is to look for an affiliate program that offers decent products in those niches. Go to Google and type in your niche word + affiliate and see what comes up.

Other Ways to Find Your Niche

There are several other ways to help you find a profitable niche:

1. **Google Trends**

Open http://www.google.com/trends and type in your niche or keyword. You will get a graph that shows you whether the niche is steady or, even better, on the rise; what you don't want to see is a graph showing you a downward trend; if you get that, ditch the idea and move on to the next one. The only exception to that is if you are looking at a niche that is seasonal – out of season, it will drop.

2. **Check to see if products are being sold.**

Quite an important point really; check to see what products are on sale for your niche. Really, you want a combination of both digital and physical products if you can although, depending on what your niche is, one or the other is just as good, providing there are plenty of choices and plenty of demand. Check all the affiliate programs you can think of; eBay, ClickBank. Amazon, JVZoo, CJ and more. You are not looking for volume, just for a bit of proof that the niche is profitable.

3. **Just run a Google search**

It's simple, type in your niche and keywords and see what other websites are selling. If they are top searches, i.e. on the first page, you know they are making some money from the niche and you know that there is a good market there.

If you find lots of products on sale, especially on several different networks, and they look as though they are selling well, you have yourself a niche. A profitable one at that, one where there is money to be made. But can YOU make any money out of it?

4. **Check for popular blogs and websites for validation**

Do this for your chosen niches and keywords; if you find lots of authority blogs and websites for a particular niche topic, it's a great sign that people are buying online and it shows you where some of them are. What you need is to be able to find these people easily so you can start networking with the site owners and drive their traffic to you. One word of advice that will prove useful – when you go into these websites and blogs, make a note of some of the content titles; while you can't use their content, you can certainly gain inspiration for your own blog.

Staying with these blogs, look for the following information:

- Do they get plenty of comments? Are they positive or negative – you can learn from the negative ones and provide the information that others aren't.
- Are these posts shared on social media?
- What sort of social media following have they got?
- What do they sell/promote?
- What sort of email marketing method do they use?

All of this will show you whether the niche is interactive online, how easy it is to get to know your audience and see what they are selling, thus seeing just how profitable the niche is.

Quick Start Action Step:

Time to pull everything together:

1. Grab a pen and paper and start making your list of ideas.
2. Once you have your list, narrow it down, crossing off any ideas that are non-starters, that don't really interest you or you just don't think will work.
3. Now follow the steps above to find your niche! Go through all the data that you pull for each niche on your narrowed down list and place each idea in order of importance. For the top three, take it further; use keywords and Google search to see what comes up and what results you see. Look at all the factors discussed above and see which niche is looking like the most profitable. Remember, a niche that looks like being a good one will have:

    - Loads of people already searching for your ideas
    - Loads of products that are proven sellers

- People who advertise, sometimes paying
- Loads of activity, such as forums, blogs, social media, etc.

If you get positive vibes you have a pretty good idea for a profitable affiliate marketing business. You may not know whether you can make any money from it but you will know that you can give it a shot give it your all, you have a high chance of success.

Chapter 5: Affiliate Programs to Find The Right Products To Sell

PROMOTION

Before you get too excited at having found your niche, before you throw yourself into getting set up and working towards your goals, you need to choose your affiliate program. Don't just pick the first one you see, make sure it fits with your niche and offers the products that you want to sell. We're going to look at three of the very best affiliate programs there are to choose from.

JVZoo Affiliate Program

JVZoo looks like a very basic program but it is one of the top affiliate networks on offer today. It provides users with an easy way to advertise their products and to find the ones they want to promote. In terms of being an affiliate, JVZoo is dead simple.

When you sign up and choose your products, you get the affiliate link and, when a visitor clicks that link and goes to that product page, their information is stored in a cookie, listing them as a referral from you. No matter how long that cookie remains active in their browser, if they go back and make a purchase, that commission is yours. And much will depend on how the affiliate program is set up. With Amazon.com, you get a commission on any product purchased by the referral but only for a 24-hour period.

With JVZoo, however, whenever a referral goes to a vendor, your link is cookied for other products that the vendor may add to JVZoo, now or in the future. For example, a visitor goes on to make a purchase using your link. A few weeks later, they decide to purchase another product and go to the same vendor. Although it wasn't your referral that sent the visitor to that product, you still get a commission, and the happens with any other product the visitor buys from that vendor.

With many of the affiliate programs, you sign up to a system of rotation payments, which means that you will be given credit on every alternative sale. If you only make a single sale, you don't get any money and if you made three, you be credited for just one. With JVZoo, you get the commission on every sale and you don't pay any fees to become a JVZoo affiliate either.

JVZoo also provides you with stats that help you to choose which products will convert the best for your niche. You also get notified whenever someone looks your way, and once the money comes in, notifications are instant. Every product in JVZoo is categorized in one of 21 categories, including:

- Food/cookery
- Finance/business
- Home
- Health and fitness
- Sports

And many others, which makes it very easy to find products that are related to your niche.

Other Things to Consider

All commission payments from JVZoo are done via PayPal so, if you can't get this in your country, you are out of luck. Plus, when you decide on a product that you want to promote, you must apply and be approved by the vendor to promote for them.

One very important thing to consider is refunds; JVZoo is very quick, instant to be fair, to pay you but, should a refund be required they will take it from your PayPal account just as quickly as it went in.

One last word of advice with JVZoo; not everything is worth promoting. Because it is so easy to add products, you will find an awful lot of junk; be careful what you choose to promote or your business will sink without a trace.

If you are interested in joining JVZoo, simply visit http://jvzoo.com

Amazon Affiliate Program

Perhaps one of the best known and most successful of all the affiliate networks is Amazon. The Amazon affiliate program provides its affiliates with plenty of great features, including multiple ways to display ads to draw customers in. Amazon also offers a minimum payout threshold lower than many other affiliate programs, although their starting commissions can be low.

To get started with Amazon, all you need to do is sign up, pick which method you want to use to add the products to your website and get going. They have a very user-friendly control panel so affiliates have less hassle and can navigate their way around much easier. The features offered by the Amazon affiliate program are numerous:

1. **Products**

In terms of products, we all know how much stuff is on Amazon so, as an affiliate, you have the ability to tap into one of the largest markets with more than 1.6 million products to choose from.

The variety of products is immense meaning, no matter what your blog promotes, you have plenty to choose from.

2. Advertising

Advertising is another area where Amazon excels, offering plenty of customization options for displaying ads. They offer widgets, automated ads, contextual links and you can even have an Amazon store, allowing you to fit the ads in with the design of your website.

3. Minimum Payout Threshold

Amazon has one of the lowest thresholds for paying out, currently $10. Most affiliate networks set a minimum payout of $50 so Amazon is one of the more competitive in that respect.

With the upsides come the downs:

1. Starting Commissions are Low

The starting commissions with Amazon are lower than many, currently around

4%. So, for example, for a purchase of $20, the most you will ever see is no more than 80 cents. However, this can add up over time and commissions do rise to 15%

Amazon does offer a wide range of customer support, including telephone numbers in Canada and the US, along with other international numbers. They also offer an online contact form, live chat online and a very comprehensive section on their website for help topics. Here, you should be able to find the answer to just about any question you may have about the affiliate program and the services Amazon offers. There is a full FAQ section and a helpful glossary, along with a section on Performance Tips where you can get help on picking the right products for promotion or finding out which types of link will work better on your specific website or blog.

To join or get more information about the Amazon affiliate program, go to https://affiliate-program.amazon.com/

Clickbank Affiliate Program

Clickbank is likely to be the first affiliate program you look at given that it has been around the longest and is still one of the most popular today. It has over 100,000 affiliates connection with thousands of vendors and, more importantly it pays on time. However, like everything, with the pros come the cons. The advantages of using Clickbank include:

1. **Plenty of Products**

No matter what niche you settle for, Clickbank will have products that match it, even if you opt for an obscure niche. There are plenty of categories to choose from so you should be able to find products that both interest you and are a good fit for your website. New products are added daily so you won't run out of inspiration.

2. **The Potential for Massive Earnings**

Clickbank offers fantastic potential for an affiliate to earn big money. So long as you follow the affiliate marketing best practices, and that includes having a website full of rich, quality and relevant content and match the products to it, the commissions are high enough to make your hard work worth it. The vendors set their own commissions but the average is between 50% and 70% per sale.

3. **Easy to Use**

Perhaps one of the best advantages of Clickbank is that it is so very easy to use and it costs nothing because Clickbank makes its own money from commission on products. All you need to do is go to https://www.clickbank.com, sign up and choose your product. We'll show you how to do this shortly but once you have your product, you can use their payment platform, their order forms, mobile checkout, their refund policy, everything. With Clickbank you get all the great features of a top-class well-established e-commerce platform at your disposal, taking away the need to set up your own online shop and payment system.

You don't have a thing to lose by signing up but be aware that you need to be very careful about choosing your product. All affiliate networks are full of both useful and useless products and, given how easy it is to upload products on to these sites, you will find an awful lot of junk on there. With quantity being opted for over quality, you will see a lot of digital products, such as eBooks and programs, that are nothing more than spam and you don't want your website associated with that.

As with any affiliate network, you should choose products from Clickbank that you believe in so take your time and go through it all. The time and the effort will be well worth it when your visitors start bringing you the commission.

Also, be aware that there is an awful lot of competition, especially where the best products are concerned, those that really do offer value. Beginners will struggle to get a foot in the door and go into competition alongside the long-running affiliates who, in truth, dominate the search results so, while Clickbank is definitely one of the better affiliate markets, don't expect it to be an easy run.

Signing Up to Clickbank

Signing up for an affiliate account on Clickbank is really quite simple:

1. Go to https://www.clickbank.com
2. Click the tab that says Sign Up and a new page will open
3. Fill in your details – name, address, email, and so on
4. Choose your site nickname which is also your account ID
5. In case you earn more than $600 in commission, you will be required to provide your business tax ID, if payments are going to your own business or your social security number if your payments are going to you as an individual.

These will only be used in the event that your earnings go over $600

6. Register your account and you will receive an email with your user ID and an eight-digit password that they assign you.

As your commissions start to generate, your first two checks will be mailed to you – this is for security reasons and to verify that your address is genuine. After that, you can choose bank transfers as your payment method.

You are not limited to one affiliate account with Clickbank. If you want to try several different niches, already have websites in different niches and want to have multiple products to promote, you can set up other accounts.

Finding a Product to Promote

1. Staying on the Clickbank homepage, click on the tab that says Marketplace

2. Type in a keyword to search for products in your niche, ensuring that you use a keyword that is your specialty and fits with the market you want to target

When you are thinking about products to promote, ask yourself these questions:

- **How much gravity does the product have?** This will tell you whether the product is popular and is selling well; it will also give you an idea of the competition you face with the same product. If the gravity is 100 or more, you have a great deal of competition and you may not make the sales you want. If the gravity is lower than 40, it may be that the product is not popular or is too new and hasn't yet been tested.

- **What kind of reviews does the product get on the internet?** Go to your search engine and type the product name in; from the results you can see whether this product gets good or bad reviews from affiliates or from customers. Try to see what the bad reviews are and what the complaints are.

- **Do the Clickbank statistics say good things?** Clickbank provides information about a product including an average commission per sale, allowing you to see whether the product would be a profitable one for you. You can also see whether it ranks high or low in total sales, within its own category and so on. There are videos on Clickbank that show you how products are tracked and measures, there are product reviews and you can go to the Clickbank forums and blogs to see what others are saying.

- **Does the vendor provide any sales assistance?** Some of the bigger vendors will offer their affiliates plenty of assistance to ensure you succeed – if you generate plenty of sales, it helps them too. When you choose a product, you will usually find a link for the vendor's website; go to it and have a look at their affiliate page. You will be able to see if they offer advice, tools, sample sales copy and landing pages to help you; the more they offer, the better they are.

3. Once you have decided on your product, click the button that says Promote. A new window will open

4. In this window, type in your nickname and, optionally, a tracking ID. This will update you on whether your affiliate program is working or not

5. Clickbank will now generate you a Hoplink. This is your unique affiliate link for use in your marketing; when a visitor clicks

this link, it is tracked by Clickbank and you get the credit for sales made through it. Hoplinks can go in your blogs, website, social media pages, emails, petty much anywhere

Clickbank will track all your sales and your commissions, providing you with an easy to see account. Typically, payments are issued fortnightly, after which you can opt to continue profiting that product or change it for another one. You can have multiple products in one niche if you choose, further optimizing your opportunities for earning potential.

Quick Start Action Step:

Below is a list of the top affiliate programs on offer today. I also provide website links so that you can look into them. Schedule a time where you can run through this list; look at each of the affiliate programs and see whether it is a good fit for your blog or website. Then focus on one which really interests you and look further into it:

1. **PeerFly**

PeerFly is an international affiliate program that takes away all the headaches, risks and costs you get with traditional advertising. Affiliates get paid when a lead, sale or other measurable transaction takes place.

2. **ShareaSale**

Trading for over 15 years, ShareaSale is fast, efficient and accurate and they have an industry reputation for fairness and honesty.

3. **Wide Markets**

A unique solution, offering cross-channel advertising allowing vendors to sell services and goods through Wide Market native products.

4. **Rakuten**

Once known as Buy.com, Rakuten is a huge affiliate network, in the top three of all global e-commerce companies. With more than 90,000 products, 38,000 vendors and over 18 million customers, Rakuten offers more than many affiliate programs.

5. **CJ Affiliate by Conversant**

The original Commission Junction, CJ Affiliate reaches out to millions of online shoppers, offering several companies under one roof.

6. **Clickbank**

Clickbank is one of the largest affiliate networks and has been for more than 17 years. It offers more than 6 million products and has more than 200 million customers.

7. **Amazon Associates**

No introduction required, Amazon is one of the largest online marketplaces in the world with more than a million products on offer for affiliates to choose from.

8. **Affiliate Partners Ltd**

One of the first financial niche affiliate markets, Affiliate Partners Ltd offers high payouts, up to $600 for some niches. They have a professional team willing to help every step of the way.

9. **CrakRevenue**

A long-term player, CrakRevenue has been offering a decent platform for many years. It has more than 700 high-quality offers and some very big exclusive offers, alongside offering cutting-edge affiliate tools.

10. **Commission Factory**

Commission Factory makes it easy for merchants, agencies and affiliates to collaborate and offers a very easy way to sign up. Their user base is one of the fastest growing and offers companies large and small the opportunity to discover how powerful performance marketing can be.

11. **eBay**

A very well-known online marketplace, not many are aware that eBay also offers an affiliate program with great tools, and the option of tracking sales and commissions and providing reports.

12. **Avangate**
Avangate is a digital commerce network with a cloud platform backing it up. It focuses on global SAAS, software and online services payments, subscriptions and online commerce with more than 4000 digital businesses on its books.

13. **FlexOffers**
A top-rated affiliate network, FlexOffers focuses on publishers and advertisers. They offer affiliates 10 years of experience, data delivery tools, fantastic customer service and fast payouts.

14. **Avantlink**
One of the industry leaders as a technology affiliate network, keeping constantly updated with upgrades, new tools, new technology and a focus on quality, not quantity.

15. **AdCombo**

A CPA network, AdCombo uses its own technology to help affiliates customize their advertising, encouraging and fostering relationships between publishers and advertisers for the monetization of traffic.

Chapter 6: Setting Up Your Blog Or Website

Affiliate marketing is a great way of generating income online and there are those who will say that it is dead simple to create a website and get started as an affiliate marketer. Technically, there is truth in that but by no means does it give you any indication of the amount of work you need to put in.

As with anything, succeeding at affiliate marketing will depend on the effort you put in. If you can find sufficient free time to keep your website or log going and come up with the high-quality content needed, you can find your audience and you can be successful and earn a decent income.

We are going to look at what affiliate marketing websites are, whether you need one and how to get started on building and designing your blog. This will only be a basic overview though; for more information on how to set up a blog, check out the book on Amazon.com "Blogging for Profit: The Ultimate Beginners Guide to Learn Step-by-Step

How to Make Money Blogging and Earn Passive Income up to $10,000 a Month)

What is an Affiliate Marketing Website and Why Do You Need One?

An affiliate marketing website is a website that you set up to promote products with the hopes of earning commission through sales. They are built in such a way that they target an audience and refer visitors to the services or products that serve them best. It all sounds very simple but getting it right can be quite tricky. Affiliate marketing is an excellent way of monetizing a website you may already have that is popular and here's why:

- **You don't need to invest very much capital.** Anyone can start a website or a blog and start publishing content even if they only have a small budget.

- **You have a huge choice of**

affiliate networks. Regardless of your chosen niche, there is an affiliate program or two to suit it.

- **It can all be automated.** There are tools that you can use for streamlining the entire process and, if you have the budget, you could hire others to create your content and manage the site.

If you have a website already then affiliate marketing is a fantastic way of making some extra cash on the side. If you don't have a website or a blog and are seriously considering affiliate marketing as a way of making cash, then we need to determine if it is the right choice.

Deciding Whether to Build That Website

It never used to be difficult to set up an affiliate website; all you had to do was set the website up and start creating your content. Things are different now because there is so much more competition in the more popular affiliate niches so you need to put in way more effort if you want to stand out and draw the traffic your way. Keeping that in mind, if any of these points apply to you, you may be a good candidate for affiliate marketing:

1. **You have spare time.** If you already have an income and you have spare time outside of your job, you can set up a website and build it up over the long term.

2. **You have SEO experience.** SEO, or search engine optimization, is one of the most important skills for an affiliate marketer to master because organic traffic will be the guiding light for success.

3. **You have experience in web development.** If you can build a website, you can save a ton of money by not having to pay some

to do it for you.

4. **Your budget allows for significant outsourcing.** If you have the money you can employ others to create and to run your affiliate website for you.

There are three qualities that go with affiliate marketing and you need at least two of them. Those qualities are a good work ethic, a lot of patience, and a reasonable budget. If you can demonstrate two of those and can fit any of the categories mentioned above, affiliate marketing is a good choice for you.

Why Do You Need a Blog or Website?

Simply because most affiliate programs will require that you provide a blog or website address before you they will allow you to join. A vendor will need you to have a website so they can verify you as an affiliate and ensure that you can meet the high-quality standards they set. Plus, we live in a digital world; sure, you can use your social media account to place affiliate links but you will get much further with a professional website.

Choosing Your Blogging Platform

Time to start looking at building a blog. Before you begin, you need to make a few decisions. For example, which content management system (CMS) will you use? What hosting provider and domain name do you want and what theme will your website have, just to name a few. Once you have done that, you can start looking at the design of your blog but we'll look at that a bit later on. Let's start with your blogging platform.

Choosing a Platform

This is your first real step; choosing the platform you will use to build your blog. There is no doubting that one of the easiest and most popular of all the blogging platforms is WordPress, with more than half the global blogs being built on it. WordPress is one of the best content creation systems but you have to decide whether to go with WordPress.org or WordPress.com. What is the difference? Well, despite sharing a common name, they are two different platforms.

- **WordPress.org**

You will often hear this termed as "the real WordPress" and is the platform you hear about the most. It is completely free to use but is a little bit on the demanding side. This is because it is a self-hosted platform; it's down to you to provide a web host and a domain name for your website.

In WordPress.org you get an unlimited number of themes and plugins, some created by WordPress, others created by developers and designers. Some are free and some require payment but the sheer number on offer makes customizing your site very easy.

- **WordPress.com**

WordPress.com is not free to use, but does offer three different payment plans plus a free plan for the hobbyist website builder; this is very limited but it may just offer what you want. Prices start at $4 per month, billed yearly, and go up to $25 per month for business use.

The advantage you gain is that web hosting and domain names are built-in to the platform, giving you an all-in-one solution. The downside is that you may be constrained by limits because you need to fit into the plan you purchase but it is all very easy to use and all website backups and updates are done automatically for you.

For an affiliate website, you probably want to start with WordPress.org because you get the flexibility in choosing your own web host and it is much less limited. Even Disney uses WordPress.org and you won't get a much better or bigger recommendation than that!

Choosing a Webhost

Once you have chosen your platform, you need to come up with your domain name and choose a web host, unless you opted for WordPress.com. Starting with your web host, there are many to choose from but one thing to look for is the one-click installation of WordPress – simply choose your host, press the button and WordPress is installed for you.

Some of the web hosts that come highly recommended include:

- BlueHost
- DreamHost
- HostGator
- InMotion Hosting
- SiteGround

When you choose a web host, some of the most important factors include:

- **What the cost is** and do you get

a free domain with it?

- **Load speed** – how long the loading time is, on average, for the US, Asian and European users over a 12-month period.
- **Uptime** – the average uptime over the 12-month period
- **Customer support** – what do they offer? Phone support? Live chat? Ticket support? What do people think of their customer service and what is their response time on average?
- **Security** – do they offer any type of security? What is it?

Making sure your web host is the right one for you and your requirements is an important part of setting up your affiliate marketing website or blog. If you pick the wrong one, you can do all the work you want and have the best CMS in the world; it won't make any difference.

Bad web hosts can affect your search engine rankings negatively and the result of that is a waste of your time, hard work and money, as well as pushing you backward in terms of an expert and authoritative presence online.

Before you choose, look at everything; look at it again and analyze everything that goes for or against a specific solution. Where possible, avoid using free hosting solutions; these are often provided in exchange for you placing a promotional link in your website footer and while this might sound like a fair deal, it really isn't worth the risk.

Why? Because very rarely will you ever come across a free web host that is reliable. This is one area of your business that you should never neglect or try to economize on. Free hosting solutions don't hang around long and signing up to one could mean you end up high and dry later down the line, with all your hard work going down the drain when your provider shuts the doors. Be smart and choose one of the paid options; the investment will be well worth it.

Choosing a Domain Name

Choosing the right domain name is important for any website and there are some protocols you should follow when choosing your name:

- It should tell people instantly what your blog is about
- It must be a good enough name that you identify with it easily
- It must define your identity in business terms
- It must be a brandable name; if it isn't actually your brand name then it must correspond closely to it

Many people struggle to come up with good names for their blogs and there are a couple of rules that you should work by to help you get the best one to push your blog in the right direction:

- It must be short
- It must contain one of your primary keywords

- It must be memorable

All of this means you need to find the right balance between a name that is simple yet unique. It mustn't be a long complex name that no-one will ever remember and it must be easy to pronounce and even easier to type.

Simple and specific means your name will be much easier to remember so don't use abbreviations, business slang, hyphens or numbers – all these just make your name look unprofessional and suspicious.

Designing Your Blog

Now that the technical side is out of the way, it's time to get down to designing your website. You want a design that is going to fit with your niche and best shows off your content. If you go for WordPress there are loads of themes built-in, some of them completely free and others requiring a payment. Whichever way you go, your blog design needs to be:

- **Simple** – as simple as you possibly can. A showy website takes attention away from your content and your readers won't gain much from it. White space is good, simple is good as your words stand out and are much more impressionable.

- **Simple fonts** – and a standard one. If you use weird and wonderful fonts, people won't read it and obscure or fancy fonts don't always display on all systems properly

- **Contract your colors** – but use only a few as and where needed to draw attention to something significant or to highlight something

- **Goal-driven** – each of your blog pages need to have a goal and it should only be a single goal. Work out what that goal is and design your blog around it

- **Visual** – use images and videos to make your blog stand out and make people want to read it. Make sure your visuals are professional and clean.

When you upload images, ensure you use the highest resolution you can but also make sure the images are not too heavy otherwise your page loading time goes up and that is never a good thing.

The average user has a short attention span so if your page takes longer than three seconds to load, you will lose visitors. Think about compressing your images and, if you are using WordPress, look at which plugins you can use to help you.

The next step in designing is to decide what information categories you need. Do plenty of research here and make sure your categories and tags are not just what you expect but match with your keywords and your strategy in terms of content.

The best architecture for any website tends to follow a rule of three clicks. What this means is a user should make no more than three clicks on your website to find the information they want; anymore and they will get bored! You should also remember that your website will need a sitemap and you need to include robots.txt for your indexing to be optimal.

- **robots.txt**

This is a small text file that gets stored on your server and it is used for telling the search engine bots which pages on your site to crawl. You can also indicate if a certain page is to not to be crawled.

- **Sitemap**

A sitemap is a vital file for any website and is nothing more than a list of every page on your website that visitors can access. Those pages must be in an organized manner and should be predefined.

Now we can look at SEO optimization using keywords and content in the right places. Title tags and meta descriptions must be completed so there are no empty category pages. These will show up in the search results so make sure they are written in a catchy manner to encourage people to click.

Using pagination or adding a "Load More" button along with a box for searching will let your visitors work their way through your site and your content easily and find anything they want.

Publishing Content

Publishing content is not quite as easy as it sounds. You need a strategy, not just for the posts you are going to publish now but for what you are going to do in the next three, six and nine months and in the next year. This way, you can keep on top of things, ensure relevant content is published frequently and monitor your results. Setting quarterly strategies is the easiest and best way because it provides enough time for a strategy to work and not too much time for bad strategies to do damage. They are flexible and can be adjusted easily if something isn't working and a quarterly strategy is not too demanding in terms of time.

With an affiliate blog, the only difference is adding your affiliate links in the right places and we will be discussing that further later.

Once more, for more information on how to build a profitable blog, check out the book on Amazon.com "Blogging for Profit: The Ultimate Beginners Guide to Learn Step-by-Step How to Make Money Blogging and Earn Passive Income up to $10,000 a Month).

Quick Action Step

Spend half an hour researching blog

platforms and web hosts; make notes on what each platform offers and what the downsides are so that you can make your decision on which to use. Take the time to come up with a top-class name for your blog and get down to designing it.

Chapter 7: Strategies Where to Place Affiliate Links

BLOGGING

What Are These Affiliate Links?

So, affiliate links. What are they, exactly? An affiliate link is a web link that takes a visitor to a specific website. Encoded into the link is a tracking cookie and your personal affiliate ID. The cookie tracks what happens when the link is clicked and, depending on what affiliate program you have signed up to, you may earn a commission based on leads, referrals, clicks or sales. The cookie will monitor how many purchases are made and you then get the commission for those sales. It is important to note that only the website the purchases are made from can see any of your information, no one else.

Let's take an example; say you click a link that takes you to Amazon. That link will likely contain an affiliate link – hover your mouse over the link and, at the very end, you will see "tag= ..." followed by a string of letters and a number. That is a tracking link for an affiliate marketer and, whenever that link is clicked, a cookie goes into the browser of the person who clicked it and it will stay there for a set period of time or until it is deleted – anything purchased using that link provides a commission to the link owner.

Now, the Amazon affiliate system doesn't pay huge amounts of commission, starting at 4% but, depending on the purchase price of the product and how many times it is clicked, you have the potential to earn a lot. But you also have the potential to earn little. Let's say that link takes you to a $2 eBook and you buy it. That earns the affiliate marketer just 8 cents and if you are the only one to purchase that book in that month, that is all they earn from the link. As is said, it is not a get-rich-quick scheme!

1. **Is every affiliate link the same?**

No. Each affiliate program is different and each is set up differently. Some cookies will count only the order for the first click while others will continue counting orders for a longer period of time. Each program has its own rate of commission, some paying a set dollar (or cent) amount per sale and others paying a set percentage of the sale price – some pay 3 or 4% while others will pay upwards of 50%.

2. **Why bother with the lowest paid links?**

Because every penny or cent counts. Most affiliate links have a set payout amount and you could reach that quite quickly if you get loads of clicks and purchases or it might take you a long while. The thing is, once you have a blog set up, that link stays there until you choose to delete it; the bigger your audience grows, the more chance there is of the link being clicked and that results in more sales and more commission.

3. **Why do we even have affiliate links**?

Because everybody wins from it. Most websites have a limited advertising budget so using affiliate marketers to spread the word is doing them a favor, once that is paid for when a sale is made, not before as in traditional advertising. Their name is spread further afield and they make more money, paying the affiliate marketer whenever a successful sale or lead is made. And that sale is more likely when it comes via a personal endorsement.

Don't think that every link is one of these; many affiliate marketers will recommend services or products that they never use to those that are likely to use them. It gives the blogger a subject to discuss on his or her blog and puts money in their pocket and that of the product or service owner so everybody gains from it.

Most bloggers will do what they do because they have a passion for their subject, because they have much to bring to their audience so why not use that passion to earn money? It costs you nothing to do it and it stands to gain you money in your bank account if you push the products in a compelling way.

Managing Your Affiliate Links

Having affiliate links on your website is one thing but when you have several at once, you should be looking at a way of managing them, maintaining them and keeping them updated. This is a critical part of affiliate marketing and there are plenty of tools that can help you do this.

When you first start, you will probably just have one or two links, just to see how things go but, as your business grows, you will add more in and you could potentially have thousands of them, both banner links and text links. It doesn't matter what type of link you use; what is important is how many you have and learning how to manage them can save you an awful lot of heartache later on.

So, managing these links – how do we do this? 90% of the time, you will add links to your content with no real intention of ever removing them so why do you even need to manage them? Let's look at a couple of examples.

Let's say that you have multiple affiliate links for one vendor, all going to different products. These links are scattered throughout your content and, in many cases, will even be duplicated. They bring you in a reasonable income but, all of a sudden, things start dropping off. Why? Because the vendor changed their URL and, while redirects were in place for a while, these don't stay in place forever. It's up to you to change the URL for every one of the links you have for that vendor. Now, if you only had a couple, this wouldn't be a big deal but when you have hundreds, even thousands, then it becomes a huge task. Use a link management tool and all you have to do is to change the URL once.

Another example revolves around when you need to remove links and any contextual text that surrounds them. You may not be aware of every post that has that link, unless your strategy is to record the location of every link. With an affiliate management tool, you would be able to scan your posts, find every instance of the link and remove them quite quickly.

Other Benefits

Affiliate link managers also come with other benefits. First off, many will include a nofollow link and you should set this for every affiliate link; some tools allow you to do this globally so you only need to set it once and every link is assigned with it.

Secondly, a link manager just makes life so much easier. Once your links have been created, you can easily add them using whatever method you want – text, banner or whatever, to any of your posts, using the Post Editor window in the tool.

So, if you intend to have many affiliate links in your content, make sure you get prepared with a link manager now and not have a meltdown later on when you have thousands of links to sort out. If you are new to all this and are just setting up your blog, all well and good but if you already have a blog that has links scattered all over the place, best settle down, get them sorted and then put your link manager in place.

The Best Places to Put Your Links

So, you have all these lovely links and you are about ready to put them into your content. You can just shove them into any old place, can't you? Well, you could but you wouldn't really get anywhere with them. On the other hand, you could place them properly and reap the rewards. Link placement is very important if you wish to entice your visitors to click on them. If the link doesn't appear to relate to the text immediately around it or if people have to go looking for the links, they won't click. Here's where you should and shouldn't place those all-important affiliate links:

- **Banner Ads**

Banner ads are not always the best place to put affiliate links because they don't always work. Banner ads tend to show up on every page if you place them in your sidebar and it isn't good practice to have these links everywhere – some pages on your blog won't need them. When you are first starting out with your blog, you want to choose high-quality links and stick with just a couple of really well-placed ones. Banner ads also don't get clicked anywhere near as much as contextual links. If you really want to use a banner, have it link to a product review on your website.

- **Product Reviews**

Affiliate links work really well in product reviews because people read them and they take note of them if they like what you have to say, they will more than likely click that link. Product reviews are also great for incredibly quick conversions and for quick ranking so feel free to review products that you use and add your links in.

Product reviews are probably the absolute best place to put affiliate links, so long as you keep them specific to the product or service under review.

- **Contextual Links**

The second-best place for affiliate links is in contact with the topic of a blog post. Contextual links are often called deep links and, when you build up your website, you should have two different content types – generic content that is evergreen – never goes out of fashion, always relevant, any sales content, maybe product reviews. Even if you don't have any reviews, you should mention the products you are promoting in your blog posts and add the links, making sure they are added in context with the content. If you are writing away and it looks like it makes some sense to put a link in place, do it.

- **Your Bio**

Believe it or not, your author bio is an excellent place to put affiliate links although, once again, it does mean those links will be on every page. But the important thing is it does works and you can use this to your advantage to make sales. Let's say that you have an eBook that you are giving away free; your author bio could link to that book and, in that book will be more affiliate links, thus increasing your potential for earnings.

- **Resources Page**

If you don't have one of these for your blog then create one right now. It just needs to be a page that lists the tools that you make use of and what you recommend your visitors use and here is the perfect place for your affiliate links – one beside every product that you are recommending. Whoever takes the time to look at your resources page will likely want to buy a product or sign up to one or more of the services that you are recommending so including the links makes perfect business sense.

- **Your Emails**

I've saved the best until last because the one place where your affiliate links should be is in your emails. This is one of the best marketing strategies you could ever use and you should be using it now although don't pepper every single email with your affiliate links – that will get old pretty fast.

Where your blog or your website is kind of held to ransom by the search engines, your email marketing list is not and you can do pretty much whatever you want with it. Those that have signed up to your email list are far more likely to trust your links than they would those in a random blog.

We'll be talking more about email lists and marketing later and, once your list is set up, you can start placing your links wherever you feel necessary; the usual time, if you are promoting products, is if there is a new product on the market that you think your loyal customers should try!

Quick Start Action Step:

We talked about what affiliate links are and how to use them, we talked about managing them and where to place them on your blog and off it too. What next? When you sign up to an affiliate program, you are given an affiliate link to use; make sure you use it! Too many people sign up to a program, say Amazon Associates, and then use Amazon.com as their link, thinking they will get the credit for any sales – wrong! Unless you send your visitors to a specific product that you picked from the program and that contains your unique ID, you won't get a penny in credit.

Write a piece of content that relates to a product you want to promote. For now, it doesn't matter what the quality is like and it doesn't even need to be that long. Practice inserting your affiliate link in different places in the content, see where it fits, where it looks more natural – that's the key; your links must be placed naturally and, if using contextual links, should only be used in content that is related to that product. Spend some time doing this and also read through other blogs on the internet and see how they place their affiliate links.

Chapter 8:
Getting Traffic

Now that we have the website, we need traffic to visit and start clicking on our affiliate links. First, a quick overview of traffic before we move onto discussing a couple of useful tactics to draw traffic in – SEO and backlinking.

Let's Talk Traffic

Is it truly important that you can boast to people you had more than a million visitors to your website in one year? It's an impressive figure, that's for sure but just why is it so important? Website traffic is nothing more than the people who visit your site; they are important because each visitor has the potential to convert into a paying customer. The more visitors you get, the more your voice is being heard and the more chance you have to build up a relationship that compels people to click a link or two in your   blog.

Although the whole idea of affiliate marketing is to make money, there is another side to it; the more traffic you get, the bigger your business grows. And as that happens, you can begin to expand the number and the variety of products that you promote; that leads to more potential income.

The thing is though, having a million visitors is wonderful ONLY if more than a couple convert to paying customers. It's no good generating traffic if it doesn't have the desired result for you so your focus must be on generating high-quality traffic. Bad traffic, the traffic that goes nowhere, can have a negative effect so you need to keep it to an absolute minimum. Honestly, no traffic at all is better than a ton of bad traffic. Good traffic is the traffic that has the best potential to convert into paying customers.

How Much Traffic Do You Need?

So, let's talk numbers. All this requires is one very sophisticated yet simple calculation. You need to have an idea of the costs your business has and its expenses, and you also need to have an idea of how much the average customer spends, or their worth.

You know how much money you are aiming to make because that was a goal that you set. From that, you can take it backward and work out roughly how much traffic your website will need. In short, you have an end goal and you work backward. Let's look at a completely fictitious example:

You have a blog set up in your favorite niche, one you know quite a bit about, and you have your goals – you want to bring in around $5000 per month.

Each of your customers so far is averaging a spend of around $30 per month and that means you need an average of about 2000 sales each month, or 200 converting visitors.

On average, out of every 100 visitors to your site, 1 will convert, giving you a conversion rate of 1% so, to get your 2000 customers, you need an average of 20,000 visitors every month. That seems like rather a lot!

The conversion rate we use is very conservative but there are other strategies you can use to boost conversion rates. For a start, you could increase your website visitor to lead conversion to 2% and then your lead to customer conversion to 4% using much better strategies to increase good traffic. That will decrease the number of visitors you need per month down significantly.

Website traffic isn't the be all and end all of the success of your business but increasing the quality of your traffic will increase the numbers that convert to paying customers and that means fewer new visitors are needed to meet your business goals and maintain them. It isn't all about numbers; it's about how they feel about your product and whether they are really ready to buy it or not.

One other important part of the equation is how you capture targeted traffic and turn those into paying customers; this widens your business opportunities and you are more likely to see the big money start rolling in.

Website Traffic and SEO

Website traffic equals money and the more traffic you get the more money you stand to make in commission. But how do you get that traffic? Well, the easiest way is to write great content because the first place your traffic is coming from is a search engine. And this is why SEO, or search engine optimization, is so important for any affiliate marketer. The main approach used is called the 80/20 approach.

What this means is that 80% of all your results will come from 20% of the actions you take; to put it another way, 80% of what you are doing has no bearing on your results. For the affiliate marketer, there are three steps to take:

1. Choose your keywords cleverly
2. Write high quality, relevant and regular content
3. Grow your ranking gradually

Affiliate marketers want their business to be automated as much as they possibly can so the bulk of your time will be spent creating stuff that will continue to draw the traffic in over the long-term. Once you get your website onto the first page of the search engine rankings, you will find that, provided you stick to simple rules, your ranking will continue to grow.

Your Three-Step Strategy to Affiliate SEO

For this strategy to work, I will assume that:

1. You have a niche that you are definitely interested in or at least have some idea about the niche you want to be in

2. That niche interests you sufficiently that you won't give up on it
3. You have ideas for content and are prepared to start writing

If you have an interest in your niche, believe me when I say you will find it much easier to write! Take weight loss for example; if the subject turns you cold, then don't waste your time writing about it; your lack of interest will show through in your writing.

Step One – Pick the Right Keywords

Competition is incredibly fierce these days, especially in SEO. Every day, more and more blogs and articles are being published and people have far more choice than ever before. There are keywords that will bring you hundreds, even thousands of visitors every month but the competition is ridiculously hard. You are not only up against other bloggers, but you are also up against the biggest and best SEO experts and companies in the world. They have the knowledge and the resources to win the battle hands down so don't bother trying.

There is a better way for you and that is to find the 'sweet spot'. This is when one keyword or several related keywords draw in from 100 to 1000 new visitors every month but do not provide sufficient results to those visitors. Target these keywords and not the massive ones and you will find things quite a bit easier – and more successful, especially if you do provide what those people are looking for.

You need to bear in mind that small and newer blog sites do not have backlinks, nor do they have a proven track record in traffic, which means they struggle to get ranked with the bigger keywords. Google and all the other search engines are looking for this when they rank your site and those keywords in that sweet spot require a maximum of 2 backlinks, if any to get you ranked in the top positions.

You could find, if you do this right, that you can be somewhere in the top 10 within a week after publishing a new article because other results are not serving their purpose – yours will.

Finding the search volume on any particular keyword is important and there are plenty of free tools to help you. Try a tool called Keywords Everywhere – this is a browser extension that is completely free to use and, once you install it, you will see the search volume across the internet wherever a given keyword appears, including:

- Google searches
- Related keywords – the alternative suggestions provided by Google at the bottom of the page
- Searches completed by auto-complete
- Searches on Amazon.com
- Searches on Bing

Getting the idea? If you can see the

volume at a glance, you can immediately judge what the keyword is worth.

Step Two – Write Guides

When you create content for a specific audience, you need to think about how you can make your information the most useful they have ever read. Guides are an excellent place to start and keeping them between 2000 and 5000 words ensures that you can cover your topic in sufficient depth without rambling. And larger articles like guides are far more likely to be shared than short posts.

So, how do we get the keywords we picked into this guide?

The absolute worst thing you can do is overstuff; by that I mean fill your article with keywords. As a basic guide, your target keywords should appear:

- In the title of the article
- In the SEO description and title
- In the URL of the article

- Once within the first two paragraphs
- In no more than two H2 headers
- And in an H3 header if it fits

Other than that, you should have a small sprinkling of keywords throughout the rest of the content.

There are times when writing a massive guide is not a good idea and Google won't always rank you well for it. Follow these simple rules and you won't go too far wrong:

- You should use long articles carefully for keyword ranking, writing only on a topic that you can write a top-class master guide on
- Do not use long articles for simple queries that can be answered in a couple of hundred words – search engines won't give you a good ranking for that

In short, don't write long content just for

the hell of it.

Step Three – Be Consistent with Content

Anyone who tells you that you can write an article and then leave it forever is a person who either doesn't know what they are talking about or doesn't want you to succeed. The content on the internet is ever-evolving, and search engines look for that when ranking.

Your content should be updated when newer, more relevant information comes along or when you think you have additional information or content to add, and that includes:

- A video
- A podcast
- An infographic
- A PDF to download
- A short eBook
- Statistics

Anything that can and does add value to

your content should be added. It must be related to the article – do not add irrelevant content because your rank will drop and you want it to go up.

We mentioned backlinks earlier. Let's look at those in a bit more detail.

Website Traffic and Backlinking

Two very important factors for growing your business are traffic and the credibility of your affiliate website but there is a third and that is search engine ranking. One of the best ways to improve this is to add backlinks. The effect of doing this properly is three-fold – it boosts credibility, it increases traffic and it increases your search engine ranking. All of this leads to more potential conversions and a bigger slice of the commission pie.

So, what is a backlink? Basically, it is nothing more than a link from one site to another. Where affiliate sites are concerned, a backlink will link from an external source, such as a blog, a forum, social media site, etc., to your own website. Backlinks tend to come in two main flavors:

- **dofollow** – allows a search engine to follow the link to the website
- **nofollow** – does not allow a search engine to follow the link

As a quick aside, you might wonder why you would use nofollow links. The reason is, they help to reduce search engine spam; humans can still follow your links but the search engines can't.

Regardless of which the links are, you can gain huge benefits from adding them to your strategy, including:

1. **Traffic growth.** Where dofollow links are used, search engine rankings will grow and incorporating these links

naturally offsite means your traffic will also grow with little to no effort on your part

2. **Credibility and branding improvements.** When you have more links that point to your site, your ranking increases alongside your credibility and this leads to a growth in your branding.

3. **Better relationships.** When you interact better with your audience, you get to make better connections.

Three Ways to Build Your Backlinks

Now you understand what a backlink is and how they benefit you, it's time to look at ways to direct those backlinks to your website:

1. Write Guest Posts

Writing guest posts on other blogs and websites that are relevant to yours is a very good way of adding dofollow backlinks to your site. You are talking to a much wider audience too and building up your own credibility. Most blogs will have backlinks in the content and, where used, the author bio. However, for guest posting to be effective, you need to know more than just where a link should go:

- Guest on the correct blogs; you can determine the most effective ones by looking at the blog demographics
- Link to your landing page, improving conversions and your search engine rankings
- Talk about industry leaders and link to them; this gives you the opportunity to share their audience, especially if your post is shared on their social media platform or their blog.

The idea behind a guest post is to fully engage the audience with backlinking a profitable side effect of that.

2. **Interaction on Industry Forums and Blogs**

One of the best ways to build up your credibility and your authority in your niche is to get involved in forums and blogs in your industry area. You will find that the backlinks will likely have to be nofollow links but you can still get the benefit of real networking and interaction. To gain the most benefit:

- Again, only go to the forums and blogs that are relevant to you and your audience
- Link to your landing page, like you do with a guest post

Also make sure you only post relevant comments and advice. You need to sound approachable and you need to sound authoritative.

3. Use Social Media

This means creating profiles on social media and being sure to have regular interaction with your audience. Some social media sites, like Google+, LinkedIn and Pinterest, will allow you to use dofollow backlinks but if your chosen sites are Twitter, Instagram or Facebook, you can only use nofollow links. However, you still get interaction and promotion and everything that goes with it.

- Make sure you choose the right platform. There are loads to choose from and you need the one or two that will engage your audience the best
- Post consistently; if you are active on your platform, you will gain a bigger audience over time and more benefits
- Track your results and make changes where needed. Your goal is to be direct and meaningful and if something you are doing isn't working, you need to change it.

Quick Start Action Step:

Backlinks are important for improving your business, for helping you to rank better in the search engines, boost traffic to your website and make you look far more authoritative and credible.

Set aside a specific time to:

- Check out blogs and websites in your industry that may accept guest posts and find out what their guidelines for guest posting are
- Check out the blogs and forums in your industry that you can become interactively involved on
- Decide which social media platform you want to use and start creating your profile – don't go mad and sign up to every platform going; you do have to manage your profiles and there are only so many hours a day you can dedicate to your work.

Chapter 9: Growing your Email List with Email Marketing

What is Email Marketing?

Email marketing is one of the most important tools in your business strategy. It is a direct marketing form that uses email to communicate a message to an audience, be they commercial or for any other purpose. Broadly, every email that is sent to an existing or a potential customer is a form of email marketing but, where your affiliate business is concerned, email marketing usually refers to:

- Emails sent with the intention of improving a relationship between a merchant and their existing or previous customers; this is to get repeat business and boost loyalty
- Emails sent with the purpose of gaining new customers or trying to convince existing ones that they should buy your product immediately

- Advertisements added to emails that are sent by another company to their customer list

There are a number of advantages to email marketing over traditional mail marketing:

- You can track exactly what your ROI (return on investment) is – done properly, this can be quite high
- Reach many more subscribers who opt to receive this kind of contact on products or subjects they are interested in
- More than half of the world's email users will check their email on any given day
- You can reach customers with personal messages that are relevant to them

The only real disadvantage is that some email providers may target your email as spam, which has a serious effect on email delivery rate. Much of this has been eliminated through the use of "opt-in" emails where a consumer will give their consent to the emails being sent and removing unsolicited emails, meaning they should only receive relevant emails that they have asked for.

So, why should you do email marketing and how do you do it?

Why

- **Cost -** email marketing is one of the cheapest forms of marketing, especially if you do it all yourself. How else could you reach hundreds of potential customers in one hit for peanuts compared to traditional mail marketing methods
- **Success** – emails target specific customers with specific information and the RI is much higher than any other form of marketing – provided you get it right

- **Measurable and flexible** – you can easily track whether your emails are successful using the many analytic tools available today. You can see what's working and what isn't, tweaking what isn't instantly.

How

The best way to look at this is to use a mnemonic – CRITICAL:

- **Creativity** – how you design your email – the color, images, layout, etc. You should ask your customers whether they prefer plain text or HTML emails as some prefer one format over another.
- **Relevant** – the key here is targeting. Your emails must be relevant to the customer and personal if you want a high response rate.
- **Incentivized** – most people look at an email and ask themselves –

what's in it for me (WIIFM?). They want to see something so offering a freebie of some description is more likely to tempt them to take part.

- **Timed** – emails should never be sent so they arrive overnight; you want that email to appear sometime during the day so they are more likely to see it and respond.
- **Integrated** – a single marketing method will not get you very far so tie your email marketing in with other marketing methods and make sure they all have the same message and the same image at the same time.
- **Copy** – when you get to the copywriting for each email, you must think about everything, from the subject to your signature. Don't save all your affiliate links for the final sentence either; get them in their early to attract impulsive customers.

- **Attribute** – this is your email header and it should include several pieces of information, including the email subject line, the to and from addresses, the date and time of receipt and the format. Again, when you test your marketing campaigns, you can see the attributes that customers consider spam and concentrate on those that get you somewhere.
- **Landing page** – if you want your email marketing campaign to generate conversions, you need to link to the pages you want them to go to, not just your homepage. If you want them to buy a product, link to it; if you want them to read a specific post on your website, link directly to it. Don't make them go looking for the information because they won't.

So, as you see, email marketing is an important part of any business strategy, especially for affiliate marketers so learn how to use it properly and your success rates will rise. Make those emails worth reading and offer information that the customer wants to read.

Setting Up Your Landing Page

Landing pages can be one of two things – ready-made or built from scratch. Many businesses use ready-made landing pages simply because it's much easier than trying to learn how to build one-plus they really aren't expensive; the more sales you generate, you more you can afford it. But, ready-made pages come with two limitations:

1. You can't do much customization
2. You need to pay out every single month for the same page – for as long as your blog or website is in existence.

Companies that offer ready-made landing pages follow a SAAS model (Software as a Service) and this model tends to make sense because there are no major expenses up front, just a small monthly payment. You remove all risks that the software investment you put in will disappear within a couple of years and you gain a certain amount of functionality that you can't afford to buy right off the bat. However, where landing pages are concerned, SAAS doesn't make a whole lot of sense unless you need a ton of landing pages and you think that, within a year or so, you will ditch them all and get new ones.

Creating a Landing Page From Scratch

If you prefer to do this yourself, here's how:

- **Begin With Your Design**

Look at any service that offers landing pages and you will see just how many there are to make your choice form. Look a bit closer and you will see that they all derive from one of a few simple templates. Three templates that you should consider are:

- **Lead generation** – a landing page designed to foster a few warm leads
- **Opt-in** – a landing page that offers a lead magnet in return for providing an email address and opting into an email list
- **Webinar Signup** – a landing page that promotes webinars and takes signups for the next one

These three pages are where it all happens and that means they are the pages that make you money. That means you must be prepared to invest in them if you want the return. Look around the internet and you will see a thousand or more different variants of these three but every landing page must have three things:

- It must have a value proposition
- It must have a call to action (CTA)
- It must have visual media

That's it really.

The companies that sell landing page templates already have the data on hand to continually analyze every one of the on-page elements but rarely will find any landing page that doesn't have all three of the above.

Designing your own landing page is a simple case of using someone else's or designing your own around the three important elements. And it really isn't rocket science; you get to come up with a great design that works and pulls in the results you want. You have two options from here:

- Do your own coding, if you know how
- Pay someone else to code it for you

If you are at all unsure about the coding and you really don't have the budget to pay someone, just use a ready-made template for now.

- **Writing Your Copy**

This is absolutely the hardest bit of it all and the most important. Your copy needs to grab the attention of your readers right from the word go. You need to push aside all the waffle they already see and get right to the point, creating an instant connection. And that connection is something you must build up enough to get the response you want.

To that end, as I said earlier, you need to have a value proposition and you need a CTA. Keeping things standard, the value proposition will be an attention-grabbing headline and a worthwhile description, maybe with a bullet-point list that breaks down the benefits of your offer for your readers, The format really isn't the point here although it should look eye-catching; what is important is what value you are communicating – benefits not function. Your customers are really not bothered what you do, they just want to know what you are going to do for them.

Your copy must be to the point with everything described or enough to make your readers want to scroll down the page for more information and keep on scrolling and reading.

- **Give Limited Options**

Not all visitors are the same and not all visitors will be at the same point on the cycle of buying. If a visitor is on the awareness stage, or the comparison or research stages, you want to give them enough information to want to learn more and you have to make it easy for them to do their research on your site. You can do this by using links to information on other pages on your site, which is where they will find your affiliate links. Do NOT leave your links to the CTA – a large number of visitors will simply leave because they are not ready to purchase yet and they will forget about you.

Your landing page is also the entrance to a sales funnel; it isn't the main door to a large store where your visitors can just browse at leisure. Every option made available should one small cog in the large wheel that drives your funnel, moving your visitors one step forward at a time.

Your visitors need to be given options but they must lead them into the sales funnel, not the Buy Now link straight away. Give them options to research more, to find out more about the products you are promoting before you offer them the chance to purchase that product.

Setting Up an Email Autoresponder

Most landing pages contain some kind of opt-in form or a link will take them to an opt-in form, where they provide their email address and consent for you to contact them by email with relevant information. The problem with this is that you need to respond to every single one of the forms that is completed and, when you only have a couple of visitors that isn't too much of a problem; when you have hundreds, it becomes too much work. The best way to deal with this is to set up an email autoresponder.

Autoresponders are one of the most powerful tools any affiliate marketer will have in their toolkit. An autoresponder will help you to engage with your list, build your relationships and make those all-important sales conversions. It also allows for automation of your sales and marketing, leaving you to focus on keeping your website up and running and relevant.

Autoresponders are email sequences, sent out to certain portions of your email list. They are triggered off by something specific happening, such as, in the first instance, completing that opt-in form. Other events include browsing your website, putting items into the shopping cart and then abandoning it, making a purchase and so on.

You create the copy for these emails in advance and set them to send when the specified event is triggered ad this is all done through the software you use for email marketing. So, how do you set one up?

Step One – Pick a Goal

There are any number of goals you could have but there are four main ones; pick one or more before you create your autoresponder sequence:

- Welcoming new subscribers when they initially subscribe to your list by completing the opt-in form. You could include links to free stuff, a word of thanks and a CTA. Set up a sequence of emails that go out at set times, for example, 2 days, 4 days, 10 days after they sign up. Each email must provide something of value

- As a lead magnet to attract new people to your list. This tends to be done by offering free courses or challenges whereby the person gets a series of emails over so many days or weeks, each with a lesson or other information.

- To make sales. For example, you could send out a series of emails containing educational videos about one or more products you are promoting, followed by a sales video and so on, to try to gain more sales of your affiliate products. Or you could send out a series of educational emails ending with one where you invite them to a webinar where you make them an offer they can't refuse.

- Promoting cross-sells and upsells after a purchase has been made. If you promote affiliate products that are related to one another, you could set up a series of email offering a purchaser the chance to buy one of these related products. Let's say that you are promoting a digital camera; you could also be promoting accessories and when the order is made for a camera, you could offer those additional accessories at the time of checkout.

Really, the possibilities are never-ending; so long as it relates to your business and is of value and relevant, it will work.

Step Two – Segmenting Your List

This is where you break your list into small groups, each based on certain criteria. It could be demographics, interests, purchases, etc. and doing this means being able to send relevant targeted emails to specific subsets of your list. The easiest time to do this in when you get the subscribers.

Step Three – Choose the Right Software

To schedule your sequence and send it, you need email marketing software and there are loads to choose from. Two of the best are:

- **MailChimp**

Perhaps one of the best known, MailChimp is ideal for beginners. It is easy to set up, user-friendly and allows you to send autoresponders for any number of triggers. To use the autoresponders, you need a paid plan, starting at $10 per month.

- **AWeber**

Generally, AWeber is much the same as MailChimp, with the same features but it does make segmenting your list easier and they have much better customer support. Plans start at $19 per month with a 30-day free trial.

Both services are autoresponders and both offer segmentation options at differing levels.

Step 4 – Map Your Sequence

It's time to set out your email sequence outline and your first step is to work out how long it will be. Will it run over days? So many emails? There are no rules; the sequence should be sufficient to accomplish your goal and no more so length is determined by that.

Next, work out how much time will be between each email; don't leave it too long though or they may forget about you. You also need to work how many emails will be sent offering value before you send the sales email out.

What is important is the value you offer, not how many emails you send but the values emails should always outnumber the sales emails or your list will burn out. Stick to the 80/20 rule – 80% of the emails you send should be value emails, the remaining 20% will be sales.

Write an outline of your entire sequence, describing what each email will talk about and the CTA for each one – this could be a link, a share, a purchase, and so on, whatever you want the customer to do in that particular email.

Step Five – Write a Series That Will Convert

This is the hard part, writing the content. If you have the budget, you could outsource this otherwise you are going to have to tackle it yourself. If you do that, keep in mind:

- Your focus is on the reader and their needs, not yours. You want to offer a solution to a problem they have, not just talk about your products.
- Personalize the email content to make it more relevant; this is more than just putting their first name in it, you need to tailor the content too, based on your segmentation.
- Make your subject lines really great because more people read

that than read the email. It must catch attention otherwise your email won't be opened and it must be enticing.

Step 6 – Monitor and Improve

Although the idea of an autoresponder is that it automates things, you can't just create it and forget it. You need to monitor email performance to see where improvements must be made so pay attention to:

- **Open Rates** – how many emails are opened. The fewer there are, the less chance of success you have. Check whether the autoresponder is right for your list, whether your subject lines need rewriting, if your emails are being sent at the right times.
- **Click-Through Rates** – are those who read your emails actioning what you want? If your click-through rate is less than 3% you need to consider your copy –

does it match the subject line, is there any value in the copy, is your CTA clear, is the link easily found? And so on.

- **Unsubscribe Rate** – you can't stop these happening but you want the rate as low as possible so make sure your autoresponder emails are targeting the right people at the right time with the right value and don't send your sales email out too early or too late.

Quick Start Action Step:

Set some time aside to start building your email marketing campaign:

- Start looking at landing pages – are you going to borrow from someone else or build your own? Find a design that is right for your site and then start customizing it to fit
- Write some top-quality copy that provides a few options to your

readers, each option moving them forward into your sales funnel

- Choose and set up your email autoresponder – start by working out your sequence of emails and write the copy for them.

Chapter 10: Scaling Up your Affiliate Marketing (up to $10,000 a month)

The most important part about affiliate marketing is getting those all-important sales and you can't do that unless you get the traffic to convert. You may have the best landing page ever, a fantastic sales funnel and high-quality relevant content but none of that matters without targeted traffic and sometimes you may need to push things along a little.

Paid Traffic

Paid traffic is one way to give your website the traffic it needs. Its targeted traffic that has an interest in your niche and is more likely to convert to sales. For this, you need to have a budget set aside and you need to choose your paid traffic sources carefully. We're going to look at three of the best ways to get paid traffic to your website:

1. **PPC — Pay-Per-Click Advertising**

PPC is an advertising form where external websites are used to market your affiliate website. Unlike some other advertising types, with PPC, you only have to pay when a person clicks the advert to go to your site. You tend to see these adverts in search engine results where users are directed to content that is relevant to them based on what they have searched for. This can help to drive highly targeted traffic to your site from visitors searching for the keywords you used.

Perhaps the best place to start with PPC is Google AdWords, a program that uses the Ad Auction process to determine the ads that get shown for specific search queries. To get into the competition here, you need to do proper research on keywords to find those that are searched for frequently but aren't perhaps as expensive or competitive as the more popular keywords.

2. **Banner and Link Advertisements**

Banner ads and link ads are the most

common ones you will see on the internet, both in plain-text format and in images in banner ads. Both of these can certainly help to draw interested visitors to your affiliate blog and one of the best things about these types of ad is that you can use them just about anywhere that you want; you are not limited to your blog, you can even use them on your social media profile too as well as in your email marketing campaign. Because banners are so visual, they are ideal for catching the eye and the attention of your readers.

Banners are also a great way of showcasing your brand and the products that you are promoting. However, the downside is that banner ads are a bit too common and many internet users don't even see them anymore. Because of this you need to do two things – make sure they are placed where readers can't help but see them and ensure that they are clear on what they offer the reader.

3. Social Media Advertising

Social media usage is growing very fast and that means there is huge potential in terms of advertising. According to research, use of social media in advertising campaigns produces positive results, having a great effect on motivating consumers and making them more aware of a brand. In the last couple of years, the amount of money spent on using social media for advertising has more than doubled, a testament in itself to just how popular it is as a platform for paid advertising.

With social media, you can directly target your audience by using your chosen niche together with interests, hobbies and specific keywords. However, because social media is so popular now, the market is somewhat saturated and, because of that, you need to make a special effort to create engaging content that drives straight to the heart of what your audience wants. And, given that there are so many social media sites, you need to choose your platforms carefully –

just pick one or two to start with – and then look closely at your customer profile to decide the best place to show your ads.

Traffic is the only way for your affiliate site and, consequently, your commissions, to grow and using paid traffic to get your message across is one of the quickest ways to increase the right kind of traffic. It will more than pay for itself provided you do it right.

High Ticket Affiliate Marketing

High ticket affiliate marketing, or HTAM as it is fondly known, is a form of affiliate marketing that brings in a commission of at least $1000. Because most affiliate programs do not offer commissions of this level, they do not require you to invest any money in the program but you need to sell a lot more to make any kind of decent income. However, things are different with high ticket marketing; because each commission is a minimum $1000, be it consulting, coaching or digital products, anything that provides an exceptional product or service, along with top-notch support and value for the customer.

However, you are still responsible for doing your own marketing so it's up to you – do you spend all your time marketing for small commissions or do you put a little bit of money in and go for the big time? Think about the ROI; this is something that many marketers don't consider yet it is one of the most important factors if you want success in affiliate marketing.

And that leads to one more thing and that is education. You need to understand marketing thoroughly otherwise your budget will be gone in a flash. Don't forget; the products you are promoting are not yours, you are just getting paid to bring the product owner the leads.

Where high ticket affiliate marketing is concerned, where using an HTAM program comes in is that breaking even on your sales funnel front end doesn't matter; the whole idea is to generate customers as quickly as you possibly can, and that is why education is so important.

Funnels and Finance

To give you a brief overview, HTAM starts with you marketing a front-end product that is low cost, maybe just a dollar or $50. It really doesn't matter if your promotion doesn't result in you breaking even. Why? Because your back-end products are what will make you the money – commissions of $1000, $5000, even $30000 are possible.

Were you even aware that, when you promote the low-cost front-end products with traditional affiliate marketing that the product owner is making high-ticket sales at the back-end? So why shouldn't you get in on that little party? Wouldn't you rather be making the big money?

So, knowing that there are high commission sales to be made, you can increase your advertising budget to draw the customers in, knowing that a percentage of them will move up your sales funnel right to the high-ticket products.

Strategic Content Scheduling

The last thing I want to talk about in terms of scaling up your business is strategic content scheduling. For many bloggers, the odd article or blog seems to be all they can manage, email marketing letters sent as and when and then they wonder why they don't get the results they want. The answer is to have a proper schedule for publishing content and you can do that very easily using something like a simple spreadsheet.

You can use this spreadsheet to track the ideas for your email newsletters, schedule the dates for when they should be sent and set yourself dates for when each one should be sent out. When the email is written and scheduled, you can highlight it in a different color so you know you have done it. Then you work your way down your ideas, dealing with each one, and even add more ideas as inspiration strikes.

You can do the same with your blog posts, your guest posts, any other content that you need to and tie it into your calendar so you get reminders.

Why Does This Matter?

Having a proper content calendar set up can be all the difference between success and failure. Some of the main reasons why you should do it are:

1. You become more efficient at creating content
2. You become more consistent
3. You get more traffic in the long-term

Content scheduling is also incredibly important if you want your affiliate blog to be properly monetized and successful. It will ensure you have a consistent base of readers as well as drawing in new readers and your content will be the main thing that gives your readers confidence in you and your brand.

Consistent content creation is the real key and it must become a habit. When you are not creating content, you are not making any money. It is hard, especially when what you already do doesn't seem to be making a difference but that is exactly why content scheduling is so important.

The Long Game

When you update your blog constantly and consistently with high-quality, up to date and relevant content, you are presenting a serious, professional front to your readers. You are telling them that you can keep to a schedule, that you can communicate what you want to say and that you are willing to communicate with potential customers. Writing is a way of sharing your knowledge as well as being a great way to discipline yourself for the sake of your business.

Long-tail traffic is important to your blog; long-tail keywords are those that are not searched for very often but are subject to highly targeted traffic. When people search for a long-tail keyword they generally have a great deal of interest in that topic and, as a result they are far more likely to convert to paying customers. The more you create content that is valuable for your blog, the more you will use long-tail keywords, perhaps without meaning to, and that leads to a higher potential for traffic.

Quick Start Action Step:

Set up a spreadsheet and start marking out blocks of time; start at the beginning of the week and block out a set time period, say 15 or 30 minutes, just to

come up with content ideas for your
blog.

Next, do the same for your email
marketing content.

Schedule set days and times to write the
content – you can do this on a daily
basis or schedule an entire day or two
just to write all your weekly content. If
you work during the week, this could be
at the weekend or in the evening.

Schedule a date for each article to be
written and published by and set up a
system of colors whereby you know
when each target has been met.

Also set aside some time to look into
paid traffic options and high-ticket
affiliate marketing programs. If you are
not ready to take this step yet, that's fine

but do your homework now and prepare yourself for when you do move in that direction.

Chapter 11: Mistakes to Avoid in Affiliate Marketing

SOCIAL
MEDIA
WORK
AFFILIATE
EMAIL
USERS
ADVERTISING
design
conceptual
NETWORK
BLOGS
CONTENT
email
IRC
marketing
INNOVATION
PICTURES
TOPIC
NEWSLETTERS
TWEET
MYSPACE
EDIT
ecommerce
HTTP
NEWS
SFTP
FTP
PUBLISH
MONEY
WWW
messages
CHATTING
internet
sharing
CONVERSATION
ONLINE
cloud
AFFILIATE
PAGES
FACEBOOK
technology
SERVERS
marketing
web
TWITTER
SMS
presentation
SALES

Everybody makes mistakes, even affiliate marketers but you can avoid the most common of those mistakes quite easily just by taking your time over what you do and taking your time to get your affiliate marketing business off and running. These are some of the most important mistakes you should avoid making:

1. **Choosing the Wrong Niche and/or Product**

As you will know from your research into affiliate programs, there are tons of products to choose from and choosing the right one is the key to your success. When you have the right niche and the right product, you will find that you are inspired to promote them and to build up your marketing activities.

One of the biggest mistakes that affiliate marketers make is in choosing the wrong product. You might pick a niche or a product just because it seems like there is a lot of money in it for you but if you have no real feeling for the topic then you won't have any interest in marketing any of the products.

To be successful, you need to come across as natural and that won't happen if your niche or product is meaningless to you. Conversely, when it comes to choosing your products, don't pick the ones that take your fancy if they are not proven sellers. You are promoting products that you want your customers to buy, not you; their needs come first.

2. **Promoting Too Many Products**

It is so tempting to click on product after product and add it to your business but this could be one of the biggest mistakes you make. Too much ambition is not always a good thing and, as for enthusiasm, save that for your content and advertising strategy.

Bear in mind that you need to monitor all these products and there are only so many hours in the day; choose one or two excellent products and see how they go before you increase – quality should always come before quantity, especially in this business.

3. **Having a Poor-Quality Blog or Website**

This is never a good thing, especially with affiliate marketing. If your website looks poor, visitors will expect your content to be poor and they won't bother. If they don't leave immediately, when they do it will be for good and your sales volume will suffer.

There is plenty of help on the internet for building a good solid website and lots of useful platforms, like WordPress that can make it easy. What you want to avoid are slow loading times, ads all over the place, a messy looking website and so on; people cannot associate that with a positive experience so even if you worked on improving it, you have still lost a fair percentage of visitors.

A few things to bear in mind are:

- Can people easily navigate the site?
- Is everything easy to see and find?
- Is the design highlighting what it needs to?
- Are there clear CTAs?
- Is one page calling for one action?
- Does my website respond quickly?
- Is it a simple design?

You don't need an all-singing, all-dancing website; it needs to be simple yet enticing; it needs to look good while being accessible and easy to look at.

4. **Not being Consistent with Content**

Your blog must be updated regularly with high-quality content that is not only relevant but up to date as well and many bloggers forget to do this. Without that content, you don't have a business as such because that is what drives your traffic. Content must be published regularly so that your visitors come to expect it. It must be of a high quality, and of enough value that readers want to share it with others, thus increasing traffic to your website. Apart from not publishing regularly, some bloggers publish content that is meaningless so think about what you would want to read before you write and publish your blog posts. Put yourself in their shoes first.

5. Not Tracking the Performance of Your Website

Many bloggers don't see the need for performance tracking tools but how else can you determine how well, or otherwise, your campaign is working? With affiliate marketing, you need to track your data and you need to optimize it. You need to see what works and what doesn't so you can change what doesn't and you need to be able to recognize patterns in your work.

There are loads of tracking tools but perhaps one of the best is Google Analytics, an easy tool to use to help you measure performance and work out what to keep and what to ditch.

6. Failing to Learn

When you get involved in affiliate marketing, you must keep your ear to the ground and your eye on the news to keep up with changes in the industry. It is the internet after all; things change almost daily, leaving you struggling to keep up with things.

It is challenging but you must always make sure you are always informed about trends, changes in ranking (Google change theirs reasonably often) and any news that could have an effect on your blog or website. Educate yourself; read guides, read the news and always make sure you are aware of what is going on.

7. Not Trying Anything New

When you launch your campaigns, be they social media campaigns, AdWords, even your email marketing campaigns, it is vital that you test more than one version of your copy. If you continue to deliver the same message over and over, you won't learn anything. Try something different, set up two campaigns and choose which one works the best.

Never get stuck in a rut; explore every opportunity you can and keep on experimenting until you are perfect at what you do. Some things you should test are:

- HTML against plain text email
- Different subject lines in email marketing
- Different blog post titles
- Different approaches to solving the same problem

Constantly revise and improve your marketing campaigns and keep on top of things all the way; only when your business is truly automated and bringing in the money without you having to do much can you sit back and relax.

Bonus Chapter: Using Social Media to Drive Your Affiliate Marketing Campaigns

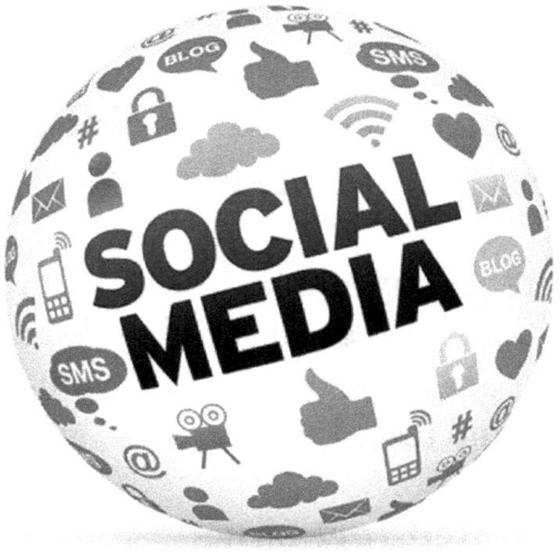
SOCIAL
MEDIA
BLOG
SMS
SMS
BLOG

One of the quickest ways to get the ball rolling in affiliate marketing, not to mention one of the most successful ways, is to use social media. However, it isn't just a case of sharing the odd post and making the odd comment; there are ways to use social media for affiliate marketing and these are the simple rules you should follow:

Effective Use of Social Media for Affiliate Marketing

There are any number of tips that you will see touted for great social media use and these are some of those that are already tried and tested:

1. Redirect Links

Affiliate links are all too easy to spot and this may result in a lack of traffic because your audience thinks you may just be trying to get one over on them. Instead of just the affiliate link, try using a redirect link; these can be made to look simple, clean and not like an affiliate link; that makes them a more attractive prospect for clicking.

Raw affiliate links look unfriendly, they look unclean and there is nothing to say where they lead and that turns a lot of people away from clicking on them. Redirects are much nicer and you can use these in any of your marketing campaigns, not just social media.

2. **Keep Your Focus on Your Content**

This should always be your first focus because this is where the money is. Ask yourself if your content can stand without an affiliate link? Are they providing value? Are they grabbing attention? Rather than going in for the kill straight away with posts that do nothing but promote services or products, start by sharing content that you think your social media audience will like

It must be compelling content that draws their attention; your affiliate link can go at the end. You can share content of all formats:

- Blog posts
- Facebook or Twitter posts
- Email newsletters
- Videos
- Infographics
- Podcasts

3. **Do Use Visual Content**

Photos and videos say much more than simple text and they are also one of the best ways to grab attention. Photos of products, video reviews, even infographics will draw a reader's eye more naturally and keep their attention for much longer.

4. **Promote   High-Quality Products**

Low-quality products will lower the tone of your content and people won't appreciate it. Obviously, you will be more successful if you can promote products that you use personally but if you can't, you should always go for the higher quality products. These lead to your audience sharing your posts and sending even more visitors your way. Instead of half a dozen cheap products, focus on one or two better ones and you will get more out of it.

5. **Stay Active**

Don't post and then forget about it. You must remain an active participant in your own social media campaign; it won't run itself. Post regularly and make sure you respond to comments. For this reason, you shouldn't have a campaign going on every single social media platform going unless you can afford to pay someone to run them for you. Choose a couple, no more than two and get comfortable with them before you move on to others. Build your audience up gradually by setting aside an hour or two per day to monitor and work on your social media campaign.

6. **Connections are Important**

There are hundreds of affiliate marketers and many of them use social media. Connect with those in your niche and support them; they may return the favor and do the same for you. Share their posts, share their links and provide a certain level of support; they aren't just your competition, you can help each other out enormously.

Growing Your Email List with Social Media

One of the best ways to use social media with affiliate marketing is to use your social media campaign as a way of building up your email list and then using that list to promote your affiliate links. Social media sites love to sell advertising space but they want only high-quality content so promoting your affiliate links directly on your social media page could see you getting banned.

By building up your email list and using that to promote your links is a much better way and you have less risk of losing your account and gaining more benefit in terms of conversions.

The bigger your email list and the more responsive it is, the more targeted traffic gets sent to your blog and the more potential money there is to be made. Always provide a whole heap of free value to your audience and you will gain their trust much easier; you can only do that if you promote high-quality products.

Social media is possibly the most powerful tool you will ever use in your affiliate marketing business. Using it the right way can provide a huge boost to your business and by following the simple tips set out above, you will soon be running your social media campaign like a pro.

Conclusion

Thank you again for owning this book!

I hope this book was able to help you to understand affiliate marketing better and see how you can join the ranks of marketers and start earning your own high-dollar income.

As I am sure you have seen, this is not an easy way to make money and, to start with at least, it will require you to put in many hours of work. You need to be diligent and hardworking if you are to succeed; it isn't a case of setting up a quick website and waiting for the money to come pouring in. If it were that easy, we'd all be doing it!

What you will get is a huge sense of satisfaction, the knowledge that all your hard work has paid off when the money does start coming in, the knowledge that you, and you alone, are responsible for your own fortunes.

The next step is to not waste another minute. Fire up your computer and get to work; the sooner you get started, the sooner you can start making that money but, and this is a big but, please don't throw your job in straightaway – you are going to need an income while you do this. Instead, put aside an hour or two a day to follow this guide and get set up – yes, I know that means working even longer than you do now but it will all be worth it and you know the old saying, "no pain, no gain". Do this properly and there will come a day when you can turn your back on your current employment and live quite happily off the fruits of your labors.

Thank you and good luck!

www.ingramcontent.com/pod-product-compliance
Lightning Source LLC
Chambersburg PA
CBHW071559210326
41597CB00019B/3309